EPISODES 1–6

BOOK
I

Family Album,

U. S. A.

JAMES
KELTY

CLASSROOM

VIDEO

COURSE

Teacher's Edition

DRAMA CREATED BY
ALVIN COOPERMAN & GEORGE LEFFERTS

Education Curriculum

PRENTICE HALL
Englewood Cliffs, New Jersey 07632

Cover Design: *Brian Sheridan*
Illustrations: *Duane Gillogly*
Interior Design: *Publication Services, Inc.*
Production Services: *Publication Services, Inc.*

Photo credits to Student Book: All photos by Eric Liebowitz, except for screen lifts from video provided by The Dovetail Group, Inc., Cynthia Vansant, photographer.

This book was set in Optima by Publication Services, Inc.

Printed in the United States of America
10 9 8 7 6 5 4 3 2

ISBN 0-02-332810-X

Prentice-Hall International (UK) Limited, *London*
Prentice-Hall of Australia Pty. Limited, *Sydney*
Prentice-Hall Canada Inc., *Toronto*
Prentice-Hall Hispanoamericana, S.A., *Mexico*
Prentice-Hall of India Private Limited, *New Delhi*
Prentice-Hall of Japan, Inc., *Tokyo*
Simon & Schuster Asia Pte. Ltd., *Singapore*
Editora Prentice-Hall do Brasil, Ltda., *Rio de Janeiro*

$\mathcal{I}$ntroduction

Welcome to *Family Album, U.S.A.,* a television series that creates exciting opportunities for you to teach your students the English language skills they will need to function independently. The series contains speaking, listening, reading, and writing activities, songs, and opportunities for individual study as well as pair and group work. The exposure to American life and culture will stimulate discussion and critical thinking by your students. Most importantly, by providing you with a dramatic story to spark your students' curiosity and interest, the series will free you to perform your essential tasks of assessing their special needs, and guiding and assisting them in their progress. The purpose of this Teacher's Edition is to orient you to the theory and the mechanics of this video-based series. Here you will find both general instructions that apply to the series as a whole, and page-by-page suggestions for exploiting specific situations as they occur in the episodes. If you have not already done so, you should read the Introduction to the student's book and preview several video episodes. Then return to this book to begin preparing your first lessons.

$\mathcal{G}$etting $\mathcal{S}$tarted

Each episode of *Family Album, U.S.A.,* is designed to be presented during three class periods. Each lesson includes a PREVIEW, VIDEO GAMES, FOCUS IN, and INTERMISSION or FINALE section — to treat one dramatic act of the three acts in each episode.

In the classroom, you might want to think of yourself as the host of *Family Album, U.S.A.*. You will introduce the program to your class and set the pace. Here are some considerations that may help you bring yourself and your class into the television "family."

Family Album, U.S.A. is a multi-level course. It has been designed for anyone who has studied English for at least one year. In most cases, the video itself is sufficient to tell the story, making it comprehensible to lower-level learners. At the same time, students at higher levels will find the series challenging. The richness of the vocabulary and expressions, and the social and cultural situations that arise in the series, lend themselves to comment and discussion by more advanced learners. Your role as the teacher is to help students work at their own level.

For lower-level learners, you may need to pre-teach vocabulary and structures *before* your students watch a scene. Help them realize that they do not need to understand every word of the drama. Encourage the idea of gathering essential information, not word-collecting. For students at more advanced levels, encourage discussion and comment. You will find concrete suggestions for accomplishing this in this Teacher's Edition as you proceed through the course.

Each act of *Family Album, U.S.A.* contains two or more scenes for language presentation, a "Focus In" segment for language consolidation, and exercises to support comprehension and provide practice of the language structures in focus. The goal of the series is to help students move from first exposure to language to independent use of it. Ideally, each class period should contain these presentation, consolidation, and practice stages. Certain activities, or "Video Games," recur throughout the course. The classroom procedures for doing these activities will soon become second nature to you and your class.

Family Album, U.S.A. is a "people"-based program. Care has been taken in the scripting to create multi-faceted, real-life characters. Their different personalities and goals reflect the values of American society and will provide a rich source for student interaction.

Most people have an *entertainment response* to television. They are used to "the tube" as a diversion from daily responsibilities. Educational television introduces the concept of responsibility for learning. The premise of *Family Album, U.S.A.* is that the two approaches are not mutually exclusive. We can both learn and enjoy ourselves. Most of the exercises call for students to view a scene or scene segment in its entirety before dealing with it as a learning exercise. You will notice the visual time code (minutes and seconds) in the upper right hand corner of the screen. Be sure to refer to the time indicated near the heading of each exercise. Play only the segment indicated. Resist the temptation to stop the video to spot check comprehension or to answer questions in a piecemeal fashion. Students should view an entire segment before beginning to complete an exercise. This will encourage them to extend their attention span and also allow them to enjoy the drama and humor that are the stimulus for learning— before beginning extensive work.

Classroom Management

Many of the exercises in *Family Album, U.S.A.* call for students to work in pairs or in small groups. Except in certain Instant Role-Plays, the exercises are appropriate for partners of either or the same sex. Students will naturally tend to want to work with a friend, and to work in groups with friends. This is not always to good pedagogical advantage. Allow students to select their own partners and groups in the first week of class, then reorganize your pairs and groups each week thereafter. If your class is multi-lingual, arrange your pairs and groups so that speakers of different first languages are represented.

If your class has continuous enrollment, bring new students into the story by having the class recap the action. An excellent time for review is during the one minute introduction to each episode, in which the main characters appear on screen one by one. Pause as each character appears and ask the students to tell all they know about that character.

Finally, a few helpful hints about the equipment: Machines are like people. From time to time they get sick. Have a back-up plan in case of mechanical difficulties. Have your students write a summary of previous action while you are troubleshooting your VCR or television. Know where a back-up system is located should yours become temporarily or terminally ill.

Thoroughly familiarize yourself with your VCR and television before you begin your classroom demonstrations. A remote control device for pausing, stopping, and starting will allow you to remove yourself from "center stage" and control the action more discreetly. Practice pausing, rewinding, and fast-forwarding to find selected phrases and to "get the feel" of your equipment. Be sure to refer to the visual time code in the upper right hand corner of the screen to view only the segment indicated. Avoid leaving the program in *pause* mode for extended periods of time. The machine will eventually slip out of pause and emit a blast of static noise. If a pause is called for in an exercise, practice until you can pause at the correct moment.

• • •

We hope you enjoy working with *Family Album, U.S.A.*, a groundbreaking television series, created to inspire English language learning around the world!

James Kelty

Contents

Introduction   iii

EPISODE 1   "46 Linden Street"   *Drama created by George Lefferts*   1

EPISODE 2   "The Blind Date"   *Drama created by George Lefferts*   15

EPISODE 3   "Grandpa's Trunk"   *Drama created by Alvin Cooperman*   33

EPISODE 4   "A Piece of Cake"   *Drama created by Alvin Cooperman*   49

EPISODE 5   "The Right Magic"   *Drama created by Alvin Cooperman and George Lefferts*   63

EPISODE 6   "Thanksgiving"   *Drama created by Alvin Cooperman and George Lefferts*   79

EPISODE 1

"46 Linden Street"

In this unit, you will practice . . .

making introductions
asking for permission
thanking and accepting thanks

ACT I
PREVIEW

SOUND ON
1:00 - 1:44

Watch the preview to complete the sentences. Choose the correct words from the Word Box. Write the words on the blank lines. The first answer is given.

1.

Richard Stewart is a *photographer*. He takes _____ of New York City on the Staten Island Ferry.

2.

Richard _____ Alexandra Pappas.

WORD BOX

the United States
meets
shows
forgets
pictures
photographer
quickly

3.

He _____ Alexandra some pictures for *Family Album, U.S.A.* It's an album of pictures of _____

4.

Later, Richard leaves _____ And he _____ something.

> What does Richard forget?

"46 Linden Street" ● 1

SUMMARY
Alexandra Pappas, an exchange student from Greece, meets the Stewart family.

LANGUAGE
- making introductions
- asking for permission
- thanking and accepting thanks
- the order of adjectives

U.S. LIFE
- U.S. population
- names and titles in introductions

ADVANCE PLANNING
Ask your students to bring photos of their families to class. They will need the photos to complete an activity on page 5.

LESSON ONE

ACT I PREVIEW

PREPARE

1. Pre-teach: *photographer, ferry, exchange student, pictures, album.*
2. Review the present simple tense. Review verbs in the Word Box and the rule for the third person *-s* ending.
3. Turn the sound off. Play the Preview (1:00 to 1:44) and pause to identify each of these items as they appear on screen: *New York City, Staten Island, the Statue of Liberty.*

PARTICIPATE

1. With the class, read the instructions.
2. Have students watch the entire Preview without writing.
3. Turn the sound on and play the Preview again.
4. Have students fill in the blanks.
5. Play the Preview a third time so students can review their answers.

EXTEND

Elicit possible answers to the question at the bottom of the page: *What does Richard forget?* (Hint: Richard has photo equipment.) Teach additional photography vocabulary: *photo bag, film, camera, reflector.* Ask students which item they think Richard forgot.

HANDS ON

PREPARE

1. With the class, read the instructions for part A.
2. Demonstrate *shaking hands* and *waving* to your class. Explain that Americans shake hands (a) when introduced to someone, (b) to say thank you, and (c) as a sign of agreement, as in making a deal. Waving can be used (a) to say hello or goodbye and (b) to signal someone at a distance.
3. Have students get up and perform all functions of both verbs.
4. With the class, read the instructions for part B.
5. Using objects from the class, demonstrate *giving* and *taking*. Tell students to give objects to their neighbors, and the neighbors to take them. Have other students ask and answer these questions:
   "What's (Student A) giving?"
   "What's (Student B) taking?"

PARTICIPATE

1. Turn the sound off.
2. Play the scene (1:45 to 4:10).
3. Have students complete part A.
4. Play the scene again. Have students complete part B.
5. Review the correct answers.

ACT I
VIDEO GAMES

Scene 1: "Welcome to New York."

HANDS ON
SOUND OFF
1:45 - 4:10

shaking hands   waving

A. People in Scene 1 shake hands. They also wave to each other. With the sound off, watch these actions in the scene. The sentences below show the order that people shake hands and wave in Scene 1. Underline the words in parentheses to show the correct actions and their function, or use.

1. Richard and Mrs. Vann (shake hands/wave). They are (saying good-bye/meeting).
2. Richard (shakes Gerald's hand/waves to Gerald). He is (thanking/meeting) the boy.
3. Richard (shakes Mrs. Vann's hand/waves to Mrs. Vann). He is (thanking/meeting) her.
4. Richard (waves to/shakes hands with) Mrs. Vann and her son. He is (saying good-bye/trying to get their attention).
5. Alexandra (waves to/shakes hands with) Mrs. Vann and Gerald. She is (saying good-bye/introducing herself).

giving   taking

B. People in Scene 1 give and take things. With the sound off, watch the scene again to see who is giving and who is taking objects. Number the following sentences to show the correct order of these events in Scene 1. Write *1, 2, 3,* or *4* on each blank line.

____ **a.** Richard gives the reflector to Alexandra.

____ **b.** Richard gives the camera to Alexandra.

____ **c.** Alexandra gives Richard her camera.

____ **d.** Richard takes the reflector from Alexandra.

BEHIND THE SCENES

SOUND ON

1:45 - 4:10

With the sound on, watch the scene again. Then answer these questions. The first answer is given.

1. How do you know that Richard is a photographer?
  • *He takes many pictures.* • *He has an expensive camera.* • *He has a reflector.*
  • *He says he is preparing a book of photos.*
2. How do you know that Alexandra is familiar with photography?
3. Does Alexandra want Richard to take her picture? How do you know?
4. Is Alexandra nervous about speaking English? How do you know?

Scene 2: "Tell me about your book."

PICTURE THIS

SOUND ON

4:11 - 5:40

Richard tells Alexandra about his book of photographs. He shows her some pictures of people at work. But you will not see these pictures in the scene. Listen carefully to Richard. Which of the following pictures does he show Alexandra? Circle the number of each of those pictures.

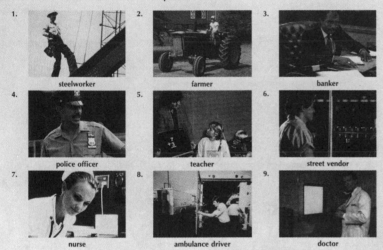

1. steelworker
2. farmer
3. banker
4. police officer
5. teacher
6. street vendor
7. nurse
8. ambulance driver
9. doctor

BEHIND THE SCENES

PREPARE
1. With the class, read the instructions and questions 1–4.
2. Pair up the students and have them observe as much as they can about the characters in the scene segment.

PARTICIPATE
1. Turn the sound on.
2. Play the scene (1:45 to 4:10).
3. Tell student pairs to answer the questions. Single-word answers are sufficient as a first response. Progressively shape responses into complete sentences, as in the example.

PICTURE THIS

PREPARE
Pre-teach: *steelworker, farmer, banker, police officer, teacher, street vendor, nurse, ambulance driver, doctor.*

PARTICIPATE
1. With the class, read the instructions.
2. Play the scene (4:11 to 5:40).
3. Have students circle the appropriate pictures.
4. Review the correct answers.

FURTHER PRACTICE
1. Review possessives *his* and *her*. Using the pictures in the student book as cues, conduct the following drill:
   Teacher: Number 1.
   Student 1: What's his job?
   Student 2: He's a steelworker.
   Teacher: Number 7.
   Student 1: What's her job?
   Student 2: She's a nurse.
2. In adult classes, review possessives *my* and *your*. Elicit from students their own jobs. Conduct pair practice as above based on student information.

YES OR NO?

PREPARE

1. Review present tense short answers with the verb *to be*: *am/aren't, is/isn't, are/aren't.*
2. Review simple present tense short answers with all other verbs: *does/doesn't, do/don't.* Review the use of the impersonal pronoun *it.*

PARTICIPATE

1. Divide the class into pairs.
2. Have students ask questions: "A, ask B about Richard. Then B, you ask A about Alexandra." (It may be necessary to replay the scene segment.)
3. Review the correct answers.

WHAT'S NEXT?

PARTICIPATE

1. Turn the sound off.
2. With the class, read the instructions.
3. Play the end of the scene (5:41 to 6:11).
4. Have students read each of the three paragraphs and circle the one they think is correct.
5. Elicit responses. Ask students to give reasons for their answers.
6. Turn the sound on.
7. Replay the scene to find out which answer is correct.
8. Freeze the video at 6:11.
9. Elicit ideas about what Alexandra could do to return Richard's bag to him.

EXTEND

Ask students if they ever lost or found something important. What did they do?

STORYTELLER

PREPARE

1. Divide the class into small groups.
2. List these key words and phrases on the board: *Richard Stewart, New York City, Mrs. Vann and her son, Alexandra, leave, photographer, ferry, photo album, photo bag.*

PARTICIPATE

1. Using the above words, elicit phrases from the class to summarize the story.
2. Select and standardize sentences and have students repeat them.

STORYWRITER

1. With the class, read the instructions.
2. Tell group members to choose a secretary to whom they will dictate the story.

YES OR NO?

IN PAIRS

SOUND ON
4:11 - 5:40

Complete this activity with a partner. Take turns asking and answering the questions. The first two answers are given.

About Richard

1. Is Richard writing a book?
   Yes, he is.
2. Is his book only about New York?
   No, it isn't.
3. Is the name of his book *Family Album, U.S.A.?*
4. Does Richard have a brother and a sister?
5. Is Richard single?

About Alexandra

1. Is Alexandra from Greece?
2. Did she come to New York a year ago?
3. Is her family living in New York?
4. Does she speak English very well?
5. Did she study English in school?
6. Is she living with a Greek-American family?

Scene 3: "It was nice meeting you."

WHAT'S NEXT?

SOUND OFF
5:41 - 6:11

With the sound off, watch the rest of Act 1 and try to guess the ending. Then read each paragraph below. Choose the correct story. Is it *1, 2,* or *3?* Circle the number of your choice.

1. Richard sees his bother Robbie waiting for him. He invites Alexandra to their house, but she says she is busy. Richard is sorry, but he gives Alexandra a bag of photos.
2. Richard sees a beautiful boat. He wants to photograph it. He asks Alexandra to wait for him, and she says yes. He gives Alexandra a bag of food, but she doesn't want it.
3. Richard remembers that he must meet his wife. He tells Alexandra his name, and he thanks her for her help. They say good-bye, and Richard leaves. Alexandra sees that he forgot to take one of his bags.

Now, <u>with the sound on</u>, watch the scene to check your answer.

WITH THE WHOLE CLASS

FREEZE!

PAUSE AT 6:11

What will Alexandra do? Tell your opinions. You will find out the answer in Act II!

IN SMALL GROUPS

STORYTELLER
Choose one student to retell the story of Act I to the rest of your group. Help him or her to remember the details.

STORYWRITERS
With your group, write the whole story of Act I. Choose one member of your group to be the secretary.

ACT I
FAMILY ALBUM, U.S.A.

SOUND ON
6:12 - 8:10

A. Watch the "Focus In" segment. Then match each description below with one of the pictures. Draw a line from the description to the correct photograph. The first answer is given.

Susan Stewart

Philip Stewart

Ellen Stewart

1. He's Richard's father. He's a doctor.

2. She's Richard's mother. She's a homemaker.

3. He's Richard's brother. He goes to high school.

4. She's Richard's sister. She works for a toy company.

5. He's Richard's grandfather. He lives in Florida.

6. She's Richard's wife. She works in a boutique.

Malcolm Stewart

Marilyn Stewart

Robbie Stewart

IN SMALL GROUPS

B. Now show your group any photographs of your family that you may have in your wallet. Tell some facts about the people in the pictures.

ACT I
INTERMISSION

PRONUNCIATION

photograph

photo (noun): [fō'tō]
photograph (noun or verb): [fō'tə graf']
photographer (noun): [fə tog'rə fər]
photography (noun): [fə tog'rə fē]
picture (noun): [pik'chər]

The word *picture* can refer to a painting, a drawing, or a *photograph*. *Photo* is a short way to say *photograph*. A *photographer* is a person who takes pictures with a camera. *Photography* is the art of taking pictures.

FOCUS IN: FAMILY ALBUM, U.S.A.
PARTICIPATE
A.
1. With the class, read the instructions.
2. Play the "Focus In" segment (6:12 to 8:10).
3. Have students complete the exercise.
B.
1. With the class, read the instructions.
2. Divide the class into small groups. Make sure that each group has at least one member with photos to show the others. Monitor the groups and encourage students to talk about their photos—and to ask questions about the photos of other group members.

ACT I INTERMISSION
PRONUNCIATION

PREPARE
1. Model the pronunciation of the words in the box and have students repeat each word.
2. Point out the shift in stress from the first syllable (**pho**to, **pho**tograph) to the second syllable (pho**tog**rapher, pho**tog**raphy). Have students repeat each word.

PARTICIPATE

1. With the class, read the instructions.
2. Read aloud the paragraph with underlined words, one sentence at a time. Have students repeat each sentence.
3. Have students practice reading the paragraph to a partner.

EXTEND

Have students practice the pronunciation of the words in focus by discussing their answers to the three questions with their partner. Encourage students to use the language in the Conversation Box.

GRAMMAR AND EXPRESSIONS

ASKING FOR PERMISSION

PREPARE

1. Tell students that to ask for permission, *May I...?* is more formal than *Can I...?* Write these phrases on the board:
   your teacher
   your brother or sister
   your friend
   your boss
   your wife or husband
2. Ask students how they would ask each of the above people for permission. Would they use *May I...* or *Can I...?*

PARTICIPATE

1. With the class, read the instructions.
2. Have students work in pairs to suggest four possible questions for each cartoon, along with two negative responses and two affirmative responses.
3. Select pairs of students to perform their questions and answers for the class.

IN PAIRS

Practice reading the following paragraph to a partner.

Richard Stewart is a <u>photographer</u>. He enjoys <u>photography</u>, and he takes many <u>pictures</u>. He likes to <u>photograph</u> people and places. He will use these <u>photographs</u> for *Family Album, U.S.A.*, his book of <u>photos</u> of the United States.

With your partner, discuss your answers to the following questions. You may use some of the phrases from the Conversation Box.

1. Do you take many photos? What do you like to photograph?
2. For a book about the people and places in *your* city or town, what pictures would you like to take?
3. Do you enjoy photography? Are you a good photographer?

> **CONVERSATION BOX**
> I like to photograph . . .
> I would like to take pictures of . . .
> I enjoy taking pictures of . . .

IN PAIRS

GRAMMAR AND EXPRESSIONS: Asking for Permission

Richard wants to take a photograph of Mrs. Vann and Gerald. He asks, "May I take a picture of you and your little boy?" Use *May I* or *Can I* to ask for permission. *May I* is a more polite form.

With a partner, play each of the following situations. In each situation, politely ask for permission to do several things. Use *May I.* Your partner will answer, "Yes, you may" or "No, you may not." If the answer is *no*, tell why.

Example: A student is talking to a teacher during a test.

1. A child is talking to a parent.   2. A worker is talking to a boss.   3. You are talking to a friend.

USEFUL LANGUAGE

In Act I, you heard ways to . . .

- introduce yourself:
  My name is . . .
  I'm . . .
- ask for permission
  May I take a picture of you and your little boy?
- introduce a conversation:
  By the way . . .

- thank someone:
  I appreciate your help.
  Thank you.
  Thanks again.
- respond to someone thanking you:
  My pleasure.
  You're welcome.

- start talking to a stranger:
  Excuse me.
- say good-bye after meeting someone for the first time:
  It was nice meeting you.
  It was a pleasure meeting you.

IN PAIRS

↕

INSTANT ROLE-PLAYS

Practice this conversation with a partner:

After class . . .

A: Excuse me. I'm _____ .
   I think we're in the same class.
B: Yes, hi. My name's _____ .
A: Say, where's room 304?
B: I think it's that way.
A: Thanks. I appreciate your help.
B: You're welcome.
A: It was nice meeting you.
B: It was nice meeting you, too.

Then complete this conversation:

At a bus stop . . .

A: Excuse me. I'm _____
B:
A:
B:
A:
B:
A:
B:

READ AND DISCUSS

Read the paragraphs under "U.S. Life." Then discuss your answers to the questions under "Your Turn."

ON YOUR OWN   **U.S. LIFE**

The population of the United States is over 250 million people. American family names—Adams, Barbarino, Chan, Gomez, Kim, Kessler, Yamada—show that its people, or their parents or grandparents, come from countries all over the world.

Many people say that America is like a "vegetable soup." Each national group is important and adds to the "flavor" of America. Alexandra is living with an Hispanic family. Hispanic-Americans come from places such as Mexico, Puerto Rico, Cuba, Central America, and South America.

Hispanics, Greek-Americans, Chinese-Americans, and other people from around the world are proud to remember their cultures and traditions. They often speak their native languages and follow many of their old customs at home. At school or at work, and on national holidays like Thanksgiving, however, everyone is "an American."

IN SMALL GROUPS   **YOUR TURN**

1. What is your last name? Is it a common name or an unusual name?
2. Does your name have a meaning?

YOUR TURN

PARTICIPATE

Have students discuss their answers to the questions in small groups or with the entire class.

USEFUL LANGUAGE

PREPARE

With the students, read through the expressions in the box.

PARTICIPATE

1. Have students close their books.
2. Give each cue below. Elicit appropriate expressions from the class for each situation. The possible student answers are in parentheses.

Teacher: You're walking on the street, and you want to get a stranger's attention.
Student: (Excuse me.)
Teacher: Someone helps you carry something.
Student: (Thank you. *or* I appreciate your help.)
Teacher: Someone helps you a second time.
Student: (Thanks again.)
Teacher: You're introducing yourself at a party.
Student: (I'm . . . *or* My name is . . .)
Teacher: You're saying good-bye to someone you just met.
Student: (It was a pleasure meeting you. *or* It was nice meeting you.)
Teacher: Someone thanks you for your help.
Student: (My pleasure. *or* You're welcome.)
Teacher: You remember to tell your friend that you like her new sweater.
Student: (By the way, I like your new sweater.)

INSTANT ROLE-PLAYS

After class . . .

PARTICIPATE

1. Practice the dialogue with the class by taking part A yourself and allowing the class to play part B together.
2. Exchange parts. Have students say part A together.
3. Have students practice the dialogue with their partner.

At a bus stop . . .

PREPARE

Say that student A wants to know which bus goes downtown.

PARTICIPATE

1. Have students create a dialogue with their partner.
2. Select student pairs to perform for the class.

U.S. LIFE

PREPARE

Pre-teach: *flavor, culture, tradition, native language, custom, holiday.*

PARTICIPATE

1. Have students read independently.
2. Read each of the following statements to the class. Ask students to say if the statement is true or false. The answers are given in parentheses.
   a. In the United States, there are about 250 thousand people. (*False.* There are over 250 million people.)
   b. People from different nations usually forget their national customs after moving to America. (*False.* They are proud to remember their cultures and traditions.)
   c. Thanksgiving is a national holiday. (*True.*)

LESSON TWO

ACT II PREVIEW

PREPARE

1. Pre-teach: *subway, lost-and-found office.*
2. With the class, read the instructions, and the questions and statements under each picture.

PARTICIPATE

1. Turn the sound off and play the Preview (8:15 to 8:57).
2. Elicit answers from the students.
3. Turn the sound on and replay the preview.
4. Review the correct answers.

EXTEND

Elicit possible answers to the question: *Will Marilyn find the bag?* (Hint: Since Alexandra asked the policeman the way to Riverdale, we know that she plans to return the bag to Richard.)

HELPING OUT

PREPARE

With the class, read the instructions.

PARTICIPATE

1. Play the scene (8:58 to 9:50).
2. Have students complete the exercise on their own.
3. Replay the scene to review the correct answers.

FURTHER PRACTICE

Conduct a cue/response substitution drill.

1. Have students repeat this line of dialogue: *Can you tell me how to get to Linden Street in Riverdale?*
2. Have students substitute these places in the response: *post office*; *library*; *police station*.
   Teacher: *post office*
   Student: Can you tell me how to get to the *post office?*

EXTEND

1. Choose other places near your school and use them as substitutions in the same drill.
2. To extend the drill above, tell how to get to each place: *You should_____.*
3. Create a four-line dialogue.
   Teacher: Excuse me. Can you help me?
   Student: Sure.
   Teacher: Can you tell me how to get to _____?
   Student: You should _____.
4. Exchange roles with the students.
5. Have students practice the dialogue in pairs.

ACT II
PREVIEW

SOUND OFF

8:15 - 8:57

With the sound off, watch the preview. Look for the three scenes in the pictures below. What are the people saying? Circle a, b, or c.

Alexandra:
a. Do you know Richard Stewart?
b. Can you tell me how to get to Linden Street, in Riverdale?
c. Someone lost this bag. Can you take it?

Marilyn:
a. Where's my husband?
b. What time is it?
c. Are you late?

Richard:
a. I'm sorry I'm so late. I had a really bad day.
b. Hi, Marilyn. I had a very interesting day.
c. I'm hungry. I'm ready for dinner.

Now, with the sound on, watch the preview again to check your answers.

ACT II
VIDEO GAMES

Scene 1: "Can you help me?"

HELPING OUT

SOUND ON

8:58 - 9:50

Match each of Alexandra's questions with one of the policeman's answers. Draw a line from each question to the correct answer.

Alexandra	Policeman
1. "Excuse me, officer. Can you help me?"	a. "Yes, the station's that way."
2. "Can you tell me how to get to Linden Street, in Riverdale?"	b. "Sure."
3. "Is there a station near here?"	c. "You should take the number 1 subway."

In two groups

Scene 2: *"Is this pink too bright for me?"*

TRY THIS ON FOR SIZE

Follow the instructions for your group. Then work with a partner from the other group to complete the summary below. Choose your answers from the Word Box. (While GROUP A watches the scene, GROUP B should not watch the TV. While GROUP B listens to the scene, GROUP A should leave the room or hold their ears.)

GROUP A	GROUP B	WORD BOX
With the sound off, watch the scene.	With the picture off, listen to the scene.	sweater green
		jacket blue
SOUND OFF	SOUND ON PICTURE OFF	pink eight
		bright nine
		dark ten
9:51 - 10:52	9:51 - 10:52	red buy
		yellow forget

 IN PAIRS

SUMMARY

Richard's wife Marilyn is a salesclerk in a boutique. She is helping a customer choose a _____.
The customer tries on a _____ one. But she and Marilyn agree that the color is too _____.
So Marilyn finds a _____ sweater. It is size _____. But the customer needs size _____.
Marilyn finds a _____ sweater in the correct size. The customer tries it on and decides to _____ it.

Scene 3: *"I had a really bad day."*

IN PAIRS

UNDERSTUDIES

SOUND ON

10:53 - 12:24

Watch the scene and listen to it carefully. Then work with a partner to act out the scene. It is not important to repeat Marilyn's and Richard's words exactly. Include these events:

RICHARD
• arrives at the boutique
• tells Marilyn his problem
• leaves the boutique with Marilyn

MARILYN
• makes a telephone call
• leaves the boutique with Richard

After you practice the scene, you may perform it for the whole class.

WITH THE WHOLE CLASS

ACT II *Focus In*

"THANK YOU" "YOU'RE WELCOME"

SOUND ON

12:25 - 14:25

Watch the "Focus In" segment. Then watch it again and sing along.

TRY THIS ON FOR SIZE

PREPARE

1. Divide the class into two groups, A and B.
2. With the class, read the instructions.
3. Position the TV so that it can be seen only by Group A. If the TV is not portable, tell Group B to turn away from it in their seats or to leave the room.

PARTICIPATE

1. Turn the sound off.
2. Play the scene (9:51 to 10:52) for Group A only.
3. Send this group outside the room, or tell them to cover their ears.
4. Recall Group B into the room.
5. Turn the sound on and the picture off.
6. Play scene 2 for Group B.
7. Recall Group A into the room.
8. Pair each student with a student from the other group.
9. Have students complete the summary.
10. With the class, read the completed summary aloud.

UNDERSTUDIES

PARTICIPATE

1. Have students work in pairs (male with female, if possible).
2. Play the scene (10:53 to 12:24) with the sound on.
3. Turn the sound off. Play the scene in short segments, eliciting the dialogue from the students. *Note:* It is not necessary or desirable to insist that students reproduce the actual dialogue. Select and standardize responses. Permit variations. You may wish to write key words on the board to cue the students.
4. Have student pairs practice the selected dialogue.
5. Once students are secure in the dialogue, encourage them to stand up and perform the dialogue as a scene. Appoint a third student to direct the action — or direct the action yourself. The director will help the actors with the dialogue and tell them how to move.

EXTEND

1. Say to the students: Now let's continue the scene. Richard and Marilyn are riding the subway home. Marilyn is asking Richard what happened, and Richard is telling her about his day.
2. Ask for volunteers to improvise this scene extension in front of the class.

FOCUS IN: "THANK YOU/YOU'RE WELCOME"

PREPARE

Divide the class into two groups, A and B.

PARTICIPATE

1. With the class, read the instructions.
2. Play the "Focus In" segment (12:25 to 14:25). Note that there are two voices in the song, male and female.
3. Replay the segment. Have Group A sing along with the male voice. Have Group B sing along with the female voice.
4. Replay the segment so that students may sing along again.
5. Instruct groups to exchange roles. Replay the segment, and have students sing along again.

ACT II INTERMISSION
GRAMMAR AND EXPRESSIONS

PARTICIPATE

1. With the class, read the instructions for part A. Pre-teach the *colors* listed in the exercise.
2. Identify objects in the classroom that have these colors.
3. Conduct a substitution drill:
   Teacher: What's this?
   Students: It's a (color) (object).
4. Pre-teach the *materials* listed in the exercise.
5. Identify objects in the classroom that are made of these materials. Conduct a substitution drill:
   Teacher: What's this?
   Student: It's a (material) (object).
6. With the class, read the instructions for part B.
7. Identify objects in the class so that students may combine adjectives of color and of material. Conduct a substitution drill:
   Teacher: What's this?
   Student: It's a (color) (material) (object).
8. With the class, read the instructions for part C.
9. Identify objects in the class so that students may combine adjectives of size, color, and material. Conduct a substitution drill:
   Teacher: What's this?
   Students: It's a (size) (color) (material) (object).

USEFUL LANGUAGE

PREPARE

With the students, read through the expressions in the box.

PARTICIPATE

1. Have students close their books.
2. Give each cue below. Elicit appropriate responses from the class for each situation. The possible student answers are in parentheses.
   Teacher: How do you like my new (item of clothing)?
   Student: (I think it looks terrific on you.)
   Teacher: Maybe someone else here saw your wallet.
   Student: (Did anyone find a small brown leather wallet?)
   Teacher: That box looks too heavy to carry alone.
   Student: (Can you help me?)
   Teacher: It's nine-thirty. I expected you to be here at nine.
   Student: (I'm sorry I'm so late. *or* I'm really sorry.)
   Teacher: I'm really nervous about the test.
   Student: (Don't worry.)
   Teacher: Which new shirt should I choose?
   Student: (Try this. *or* How about this?)

INSTANT ROLE-PLAYS

In a shoe store...
PARTICIPATE

1. Practice the dialogue with the class by taking part A yourself and allowing the class to play part B together.
2. Exchange parts. Have students say part A together.
3. Have students practice the dialogue with their partner.

WITH THE WHOLE CLASS

ACT II
INTERMISSION

GRAMMAR AND EXPRESSIONS: The Order of Adjectives

Richard lost a **blue canvas bag**. The order of adjectives is **COLOR** before **MATERIAL**.

COLOR	MATERIAL
green	woolen
blue	canvas
red	cotton
yellow	paper
brown	wooden
purple	metal
pink	glass
orange	leather
tan	plastic
black	silk
white	nylon
gray	rubber

A. Do you know the meaning of all the adjectives in the two lists at the left? With your teacher's help, try to find *things in your classroom* to show an example of each adjective of color and material. Say sentences with *one* adjective. Example: This is a **red shirt**. Here's a **wooden desk**.

B. Now use *two* adjectives to describe things in your classroom. Example: This is a **red cotton shirt**. Here's a **brown wooden desk**.

C. Adjectives of **SIZE** (big, small, large, little, medium-sized) come *before* color and material (**SIZE + COLOR + MATERIAL**). Richard lost a **small blue canvas bag**. Now use *three* adjectives to describe things. Tell the size, the color, and the material.

USEFUL LANGUAGE

In Act II, you heard ways to...

- describe something:
  a small canvas bag
- compliment someone:
  I think it looks terrific on you.
- make suggestions:
  Try this (sweater).
  How about green?

- apologize:
  I'm sorry I'm so late.
  I'm really sorry.
- ask for help:
  Can you help me?
- reassure someone:
  Don't worry.

- ask if someone found something:
  Did anyone find a small canvas bag?

IN PAIRS

INSTANT ROLE-PLAYS

Practice these conversations with a partner:

In a shoe store...

A: I need a new pair of shoes.
B: What size do you take?
A: Size ____. How about these tan ones?
B: I think they'll look terrific on you.

In a restaurant...

A: Can you help me?
B: What's the problem?
A: I lost a black leather purse. Did anyone find it?
B: No, I'm really sorry.
A: Oh no!
B: Don't worry. Someone might find it. What's your name and address?

Then complete these conversations:

At a fashion boutique...

A: I'm looking for a gift for my ____.
B:
A:
B:

At a lost-and-found office...

A: Excuse me. I lost a(n) ____.
B: Where did you lose it?
A:
B:
A:
B:

INSTANT ROLE-PLAYS (*continued*)

At a fashion boutique...
PARTICIPATE

1. Have students create a dialogue with their partner.
2. Select student pairs to perform for the class.

In a restaurant...
PARTICIPATE

1. Practice the dialogue with the class by taking part A yourself and allowing the class to play part B together.
2. Exchange parts. Have students say part A together.
3. Have students practice the dialogue with their partner.

At a lost-and-found office...
PARTICIPATE

1. Have students create a dialogue with their partner.
2. Select student pairs to perform for the class.

ACT III
PREVIEW

14:31 - 15:02

Watch the preview to complete the sentences. Listen carefully to Philip, Richard, and Ellen. Write their words on the blank lines.

Philip: Robbie, the dinner _____.

Richard: I keep thinking about _____.

Ellen: Don't worry, Richard. _____.

ACT III
VIDEO GAMES

Scene 1: *"What's Robbie cooking for dinner?"*
THE RIGHT ORDER

IN PAIRS

SOUND ON
15:03 - 16:04

Watch the scene. Then work with a partner to say Philip and Ellen's dialogue in the right order.

PHILIP	ELLEN

___ I hope it's pasta.

___ And what's Robbie cooking for dinner?

___ I'm tired and hungry.

___ All right. Is Susan coming?

___ Well, Marilyn and Richard called. They'll be here soon, and then we'll eat.

___ It's a surprise.

___ Well, she'll be here later. She has to work late tonight.

___ How are you?

LESSON THREE
ACT III PREVIEW

PREPARE
1. Pre-teach: *terrific*, *upset*.
2. With the class, read the instructions and the incomplete lines of dialogue below.

PARTICIPATE
1. Play the Preview (14:31 to 15:02).
2. Have students complete the sentences.
3. Replay the Preview if necessary.
4. Review the correct answers.

THE RIGHT ORDER

PREPARE
1. Divide the class into pairs.
2. Pre-teach: *teaspoon*, *medicine*, *surprise*, *pasta*.
3. With the class, read the instructions.

PARTICIPATE
1. Play the scene (15:03 to 16:04). Have students complete the exercise in pairs.
2. Replay the scene to review the correct answers.
3. Have student pairs practice the dialogue together.

TABLE TALK

PREPARE

1. Choose six students with differing physical characteristics and clothing.
2. Ask the six students to stand up, say their names, and remain standing for one minute.
3. Have the rest of the class observe the appearance of the students who are standing.
4. Have the six students sit down. Make statements about the appearance of the students who were standing. For each description, ask the class to identify the correct student by name. For example:

    Teacher: She's wearing a green dress.
    Student: (names the correct student)
    Teacher: He's got brown hair.
    Student: (names the correct student)
    Teacher: He's tall.
    Student: (names the correct student)
    Teacher: She's got blue eyes.
    Student: (names the correct student)

5. Repeat step 4 above, but have different students provide the descriptions.

PARTICIPATE

1. Divide the class into groups of six.
2. With the class, read the instructions and question 1.
3. Write these names on pieces of paper: *Philip, Richard, Robbie, Ellen, Susan, Marilyn*. Make a set of names for each group. Fold the papers and have each student choose a paper. Have the students look at the name and not show it to the other members of the group.
4. Play the scene (16:05 to 17:07).
5. Have the students write four statements about their character.
6. Students in each group take turns reading the statements about their character. The other students will try to guess which character it is. The first group to identify all six characters wins the game.
7. With the class, read questions 2 and 3.
8. Have the students work in the same groups, with the same character from the previous game. Have them answer questions 2 and 3 together.
9. Play the scene (16:05 to 17:07) with the sound on.
10. Review the answers.

IN FACT

PARTICIPATE

1. With the class, read the instruction line.
2. Complete the exercise in pairs or as a class.
3. Replay the scene segment as necessary.
4. Review the correct answers.

GUESS THE QUESTIONS

PARTICIPATE

1. With the class, read the instructions.
2. Have students complete the exercise. Go around the class to check on individual progress, and help students when needed.
3. Play the scene (17:08 to 20:36).
4. Review the correct answers.

Scene 2: "What's for dessert?"

IN SMALL GROUPS

TABLE TALK
SOUND OFF

16:05 - 17:07

With the sound off, watch the scene. Choose one member of the Stewart family. Watch him or her carefully. Tell your group about the person you watched. Use the following questions to help with your description.

1. What does he or she look like? (Age? Hair color? Clothing?)
2. What did he or she do in this scene?
3. What do you think he or she said?

IN FACT
SOUND ON

IN PAIRS

16:05 - 17:07

Now, with the sound on, watch the scene. Then complete this activity with a partner. Take turns asking and answering the questions. If your answer is *no*, give the correct answer. The first two answers are given.

1. Did Ellen cook dinner? *No, she didn't. Robbie cooked dinner.*
2. Was the dinner delicious? *Yes, it was.*
3. Did Robbie make a cake for dessert?
4. Is there ice cream in the freezer?
5. Are there three flavors of ice cream?
6. Does Robbie like coffee ice cream?
7. Did Richard lose eight rolls of film?
8. Did Ellen ask Susan to help her?
9. Does Ellen think that someone will find Richard's film?

Scene 3: "Nice to meet you, Alexandra."

ON YOUR OWN

GUESS THE QUESTIONS
SOUND ON

17:08 - 20:36

Before you watch the scene, guess each of Philip's questions in his conversation with Alexandra. Write your answers on the blank lines. Then watch the scene to find out the answers.

Philip: So, you're an exchange student. Where _____ ?
Alexandra: At the Bronx High School of Science.
Philip: Oh, that's a very good school. What _____ ?
Alexandra: Biology and mathematics. Richard tells me you're a doctor.
Philip: Yes, a pediatrician. And what _____ ?
Alexandra: He's a lawyer, in Thessaloniki.

IN SMALL GROUPS

BEHIND THE SCENES

Discuss your answers to the following questions. Explain your opinions.

1. How does Robbie feel about Alexandra? How does he show his feelings?
2. Is his family angry, happy, or amused at Robbie's reaction to Alexandra? How do they show their feelings?
3. Did Alexandra leave her bag by accident or on purpose? What do you think?

BEHIND THE SCENES

1. With the class, read the instructions.
2. Replay the scene.
3. Complete the discussion activity with the whole class.

IN SMALL GROUPS

ACT III
INTRODUCTIONS

SOUND ON

20:37 - 22:40

Watch the "Focus In" segment. Then work with a small group. Pretend you are all at a party. Introduce yourself and other people in your group. Respond to the introductions and start a conversation. Use the expressions in the boxes below. In your conversations, tell some interesting and true information about your life.

TO INTRODUCE YOURSELF My name is _____. I'm _____. TO INTRODUCE SOMEONE ELSE This is _____. I'd like you to meet _____.	TO RESPOND TO AN INTRODUCTION It's nice/good/a pleasure to meet you. Hi. Hello. How do you do? (formal) TO SAY GOOD-BYE AFTER A FIRST MEETING It was nice/good/a pleasure meeting you.

ACT III
FINALE

USEFUL LANGUAGE

In Act III, you heard ways to . . .

- introduce someone:
  Let me introduce you.
  This is . . .
- respond to an introduction:
  How do you do?
  It's nice to meet you.
- correct yourself:
  It's Richard's film! I
  mean, Alexandra Pappas.

- offer:
  Would you like something to eat?
  Would you like to call home?
  Can I drive you home?
- thank someone:
  I'm so glad you took the time
  and trouble to return (the bag).
- respond to thanks:
  It was no trouble.

- accept an offer:
  I'd appreciate that.
- refuse an offer:
  No, thanks.

IN SMALL GROUPS

TELEPLAYS

A. With your group, imagine that you are sitting around a dinner table with other members of your family. Talk about the day's events. While you are talking, the doorbell rings. Who is at the door?

B. Be TV writers. Write some of your dinnertime dialogue. Then practice your dialogue and perform it for the whole class.

FOCUS IN: INTRODUCTIONS

PARTICIPATE

1. Play the "Focus In" segment (20:37 to 22:40).
2. With the class, read the instructions.
3. Divide the class into groups of five or six.
4. Have one group go to the front of the class. Have them stand in a circle with the teacher in the center:

$$\begin{array}{ccc} & A & \\ F & & B \\ & T & \\ E & & C \\ & D & \end{array}$$

5. Create a three-line dialogue. (Use students' names in place of the letters):
   Teacher: A, I'd like you to meet D.
                    D, this is A.
   A: Nice to meet you, D.
   D: How do you do, A?
6. Introduce B to E and C to F. Then have another student in the group stand in the center of the wheel to make the introductions.
7. Have all the students stand up in their groups to introduce each other in the same way.

EXTEND

Have students extend the introduction into a short conversation by telling where they are from and/or what they do for a living:

I'm from _____. How about you?
I'm from _____. What do you do?
I _____.

ACT III FINALE
USEFUL LANGUAGE

PREPARE

With the students, read through the expressions in the box.

PARTICIPATE

1. Have students close their books.
2. Give each cue below. Elicit appropriate responses from the class for each situation. The possible student answers are in parentheses.
   Teacher: I'm hungry.
   Student: (Would you like something to eat?)
   Teacher: It's late. My friends are expecting me.
   Student: (Would you like to call home?)
   Teacher: Thanks for helping me.
   Student: (It was no trouble.)
   Teacher: Would you like a cup of coffee?
   Student: (No thanks.   *or*   I'd appreciate that.)

TELEPLAYS

1. Divide the class into small groups. With the class, read the instructions for part A and have each group complete the exercise.
2. Have the students work in the same groups. Appoint one student in each group to be a secretary and have students complete the exercise.

U.S. LIFE

PREPARE
Pre-teach: *title, formal, impolite, comfortable, especially, judges, college officials, military officers, clergy, occupational, dean.*

PARTICIPATE
1. Have students read independently.
2. Ask each of the following questions. The answers are given in parentheses.
   a. Are Americans usually informal? (Yes.)
   b. Can you call a woman *ma'am* if you don't know her name? (Yes.)
   c. What job titles can you use with a last name? (Doctor, Judge, Dean, Captain, and Father.)

YOUR TURN
Have students discuss their answers to the questions in small groups or with the entire class.

STORYWRITER
1. With the class, read the instructions.
2. Have students choose which of the subjects they wish to write about.
3. Give students ten minutes to write.
4. Have students exchange papers. Ask for volunteers to stand up and read their classmate's paper aloud.

READ AND DISCUSS

Read the paragraphs under "U.S. Life." Then discuss your answers to the questions under "Your Turn."

ON YOUR OWN

U.S. LIFE

When Richard Stewart introduced his family to Alexandra Pappas, he said, "This is my wife Marilyn . . . . And this is my mother, Ellen Stewart. . . .and my father, Dr. Philip Stewart."

Americans usually make introductions with first names and last names. They usually don't use *Mr., Mrs., Ms.,* or *Miss* in an introduction because they feel that these titles are very formal. In fact, if someone calls an American *Mr., Mrs., Ms.,* or *Miss,* he or she usually says, "Please call me Dave (or Jane or Sandra)." Americans usually call *you* by your first name right away, too. When they use first names, they are being friendly, not impolite.

But if you are not comfortable with calling someone by his or her first name, especially an older person, don't! Alexandra says, "Thanks, Mrs. Stewart."

Medical doctors, judges, college officials, military officers, and clergy are usually addressed with an *occupational title,* however. Examples of occupational titles are *Dr.* Stewart, *Judge* Brown, *Dean* Rafer, *Captain* Snyder, and *Father* O'Hara.

Of course you can always be very polite and call a man *Sir* or a woman *Ma'am* if you are not sure of his or her name.

IN SMALL GROUPS

YOUR TURN

1. Do you feel comfortable with using someone's first name immediately?
2. Do you think young people should call older people by their first name?
3. How do you feel when someone you don't know well uses your first name?

ON YOUR OWN

STORYWRITER

By yourself, write about one of the following:

- Write the story of this episode for someone who didn't see it.
- Describe the Stewart family. How are they different from your own family?
- Write about something important that *you* once lost.
- Write about the first time you met someone you like very much.

EPISODE 2

"The Blind Date"

In this unit, you will practice . . .
asking for and giving directions
apologizing and accepting apologies
ordering food in a restaurant

ACT I
PREVIEW

SOUND ON
24:50 - 25:25

Watch the preview to complete the sentences. Choose the correct words from the Word Box. Write the words on the blank lines. The first answer is given.

1.

Susan Stewart and Harry Bennett *don't* know each *other*. They have a dinner _____ tonight.

WORD BOX
date
very
lost
other
Excuse
looking

3.

He's _____ somewhere in New York City.

2.

But Harry is late, _____ late.

4.

"_____ me, ma'am, I'm _____ for 83 Wooster Street."

Will Harry find Susan's apartment?

"The Blind Date" ● 15

SUMMARY
Harry Bennett goes on a blind date with Susan Stewart.

LANGUAGE
- asking for and giving directions
- ordering food in a restaurant
- apologizing and accepting apologies
- occupations

U.S. LIFE
- asking for information
- dating

ADVANCE PLANNING
1. Draw a map, or grid, of the neighborhood around the school, and indicate several landmarks. If possible, duplicate the map for each student; otherwise, prepare the map for yourself so that you may copy it onto the board for the EXTEND activity on page 18.
2. Research some useful telephone numbers in your area, such as those for: emergency services, local telephone information, long-distance telephone information, your school's main office, the local public library, and the number for the correct time.
3. Ask students to bring a copy of the menu from their favorite restaurant. The menus will be used for an activity on page 25.

LESSON ONE

ACT I PREVIEW

PREPARE
Pre-teach: *dinner date, lost.*

PARTICIPATE
1. With the class, read the instructions.
2. Have students watch the entire Preview (24:50 to 25:25) without writing.
3. Have students fill in the blanks.
4. Play the preview again so students can review their answers.

EXTEND
1. Write these phrases about Harry on the board:
   - He's lost.
   - He's late.
   - He's wearing a suit.
   - He's bringing flowers.
2. Ask students:
   a. What kind of person is Harry?
   b. What will Susan think of him?
   c. Will Harry find Susan's apartment?

RIGHT OR LEFT?

PREPARE

Pre-teach: *address, breast pocket, street vendor, point, dial* (a telephone), *push, buzzer.* Demonstrate *right* and *left,* and *on the right, on the left.*

PARTICIPATE

1. With the class, read the instructions.
2. Turn the sound off and play the scene (25:26 to 28:00).
3. Have students complete the exercise.
4. Replay the scene, pausing where necessary, to review the correct answers.

STREET TALK

PREPARE

Pre-teach: *street corner, bottom floor/top floor* (of a building), *traffic light, (city) blocks, left/right turn.*

PARTICIPATE

1. With the class, read the instructions.
2. Turn the sound on and play the scene again.
3. Have students complete the exercise.
4. Replay the scene, pausing where necessary, to review the answers.

ACT I
VIDEO GAMES

Scene 1: "Can you help me?"

RIGHT OR LEFT?

SOUND OFF
25:26 - 28:00

To follow directions, you need to know your right from your left. Read the sentences below. Then, with the sound off, watch the scene. For each sentence, <u>underline</u> the word *right* or *left* in parentheses.

1. Harry looks at the address in his (right/left) hand and puts it in his (right/left) breast pocket.
2. The street vendor points with his (right/left) hand.

3. Harry takes the address from his (right/left) pocket and dials the telephone with his (right/left) hand.
4. Harry pushes the buzzer to Susan's apartment with his (right/left) hand and holds the flowers with his (right/left) hand.

STREET TALK

SOUND ON
25:26 - 28:00

With the sound on, watch the scene again. Then complete the following sentences from the scene. Use the words and pictures at the bottom of the page to help you write the answers.

1. **Harry:** Where is 83 Wooster _____?
2. **Vendor:** Walk to the _____. Then make a _____. Then walk two _____ to the _____.
3. **Susan:** I'm on the _____.

corner

street

left turn

blocks

top floor

traffic light

Scene 2: "Sorry I'm late."

MAKE A MATCH

SOUND OFF

28:01 - 29:49

With the sound off, watch the video. Then follow the instructions for your group.

Group A

Match each sentence below with one of the pictures. Write the number of the correct sentence in the circle at the top left of each picture.

1. Susan introduces Marilyn and Harry.
2. Harry asks Susan for the telephone number of the restaurant.
3. Harry apologizes for being late and gives Susan the flowers.
4. Susan meets Harry.

Group B

Match each of the four dialogues below with one of the pictures. Write the letter of the correct dialogue in the box at the top right of each picture.

a. **Susan:** Oh, I'd like you to meet my sister-in-law Marilyn. Marilyn Stewart, this is Harry Bennett.

 Harry: Pleased to meet you.

b. **Harry:** Do you know the phone number of the restaurant? I'd like to call home and leave the number with the baby-sitter.

 Susan: Sure. The number is 555-1720.

c. **Susan:** Hello, Harry. It's nice to meet you.

 Harry: Nice to meet you, Susan.

d. **Harry:** Sorry I'm late. The traffic. The parking. I was lost.

 Susan: What pretty flowers! Thank you. Oh, please come in. Don't worry about being late. It's fine.

IN PAIRS

With the sound on, watch the scene again. Check your work with a partner from the other group. Then say the four dialogues above in the correct order.

MAKE A MATCH

PREPARE

1. Pre-teach: *introduce, apologize, sister-in-law, baby-sitter.*
2. Divide the class into two groups, A and B.

PARTICIPATE

1. Turn the sound off and play the scene (28:01 to 29:49).
2. With Group A, read the instructions and statements 1–4 in the box at the left. Have Group A complete the exercise.
3. With Group B, read the instructions and the dialogues in the box at the right. Have Group B complete the exercise.
4. Replay the scene with the sound on.
5. Have each student work with a partner from the other group. Have each pair practice the dialogue in box B—in the correct order.
6. Ask for volunteers to play the scene in front of the class. The teacher or another student may play Marilyn's part in the scene.

FIRST IMPRESSIONS

PARTICIPATE

1. With the class, read the instructions.
2. Replay the scene (25:26 to 29:49).
3. Have students work in pairs (Student A and Student B). Instruct them to complete the exercise in the following way: Student A asks the questions about Harry to Student B. Student B asks the questions about Susan to Student A.
4. Review the answers. Write alternative answers on the board.

EXTEND

Ask for student volunteers to stand up in front of the class. What first impressions does the class have about them? Find out if these impressions are accurate.

FOCUS IN: FOLLOWING DIRECTIONS

PARTICIPATE

1. With the class, read the instructions.
2. Play the "Focus In" segment (29:50 to 31:49).
3. Have students work in pairs to complete the exercise.
4. Review the answers.

EXTEND

1. On the board, draw a map, or grid, representing the neighborhood around your school. Orally, give directions from the school to other places in the neighborhood, without naming the destination. After listening to the directions, ask students where they are.
2. Have students orally give the class directions to other places in the neighborhood. If you have been able to duplicate the map for each student, have the class do this activity in pairs.

FIRST IMPRESSIONS

IN PAIRS

SOUND ON

25:26 - 29:49

What do you think about Harry and Susan? With the sound on, watch Act I again to answer the following questions. Explain the reasons for your answers. Two answers are given.

Harry

1. Is Harry a polite person?
   Yes, he is—because he's bringing flowers to Susan.
2. Does Harry live in Susan's neighborhood?
3. Does Harry follow directions very well?
4. Was Harry married before?

Susan

1. Is Susan very upset?
   No, she isn't—because she doesn't mind that Harry was late.
2. What is Susan wearing? What does this tell you about her?
3. Does Susan do a lot of cooking at home?
4. Will Susan like Harry?

ACT I
FOLLOWING DIRECTIONS

IN PAIRS

SOUND ON

29:50 - 31:49

Watch the "Focus In" segment. Then work with a partner. One of you will be Student A. The other will be Student B.

- Student A will read the directions for MAP 1 to Student B, while Student B will follow the directions on the map.
- Student B will read the directions for MAP 2 to Student A, while Student A will follow the directions on the map.

MAP 1

Turn left at the first corner. Go two blocks and turn right. Then go one block and turn left. Go one block and turn left again. Then go three blocks and turn left. Where are you? At the school, the bus stop, or the library?

MAP 2

Turn right at the second corner. Go two blocks and turn right again. Go one block and turn left. Go another block and turn right. Turn right at the first corner and go to the end of the street. Where are you? At the post office, the shopping center, or the movie theater?

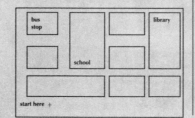

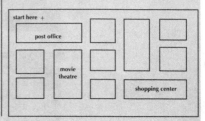

ACT I
INTERMISSION

PRONUNCIATION: Telephone numbers

You always pronounce the *first three numbers* of a telephone number by saying one number at a time. But you can say the *last four numbers* individually *or* in two parts. In scene 2, Susan and Harry said the restaurant telephone number in the following ways:

Susan said the last four numbers in two parts:

Susan: The number is five five five . . . **seventeen twenty. (17-20)**

Then Harry *verified* the number—he repeated it to be sure he understood. He said the last four numbers individually:

Harry: Five five five . . . **one seven two oh. (1 - 7 - 2 - 0)**

IN PAIRS

A. With a partner, read the following conversation. Then practice the conversation by using the telephone numbers of the four places below.

Student A: Do you know the phone number of the **bookstore**?
Student B: Sure. It's six seven four . . . **eighty-eight forty-five.**
Student A: Six seven four . . . **eight eight four five**?
Student B: Yes, that's right.

THEATER	SKATING RINK	GAS COMPANY	BOOKSTORE

395-5687	504-2390	611-1514	674-8845

IN SMALL GROUPS

B. Do you know the following important telephone numbers in your area? Work in a small group to find out. Say each number if you know it.

1. emergency services (police/ambulance/fire)
2. local telephone information
3. long-distance telephone information
4. your school's main office
5. the local public library
6. the number for the correct time

ACT I INTERMISSION
PRONUNCIATION

PREPARE

1. Write these three groups of numbers on the board:
   1-2-3-4   1-4-6-8   3-5-2-1
2. Have students say the numbers in each group individually.
3. Erase the first and last hyphens in each group:
   12-34   14-68   35-21
4. Have students say the numbers in two parts. Tell the class that these are the two ways to pronounce the last four numbers of a telephone number.

PREPARE

1. With the class, read the instructions. Model the pronunciation of the examples (Susan's and Harry's) and have the class repeat.
2. Read the instructions for part A and have two students model the four-line dialogue for the class.
3. Have students work in pairs to practice the conversation by substituting the other places and telephone numbers.
4. Ask for partners to volunteer to perform one of the substitutions for the class.
5. With the class, read the instructions for part B. Have students work in small groups to complete the activity.

FURTHER PRACTICE

1. Practice saying numbers that end with two zeros (555-4300: *Five five five . . . four three hundred* or *Five five five . . . four three oh oh*).
2. Practice saying numbers that end with three zeros (555-4000: *Five five five . . . four thousand*).

GRAMMAR AND EXPRESSIONS

PREPARE

With the class, read through the explanation in the box at the top of the page.

PARTICIPATE

1. Make these statements to the class to elicit apologies using the forms in the Conversation Box at the bottom of the page.
   - "Ouch! You stepped on my toe!"
   - "Oh! You pushed me!"
   - "Oh, no! You spilled coffee on my rug!"
   - "What? You lost my book?"
2. With the class, read the instructions.
3. Have students work in pairs to create two lines of dialogue for each of the cartoons. One student will think of an apology and an excuse, and the other will think of an acceptance.
4. Ask for volunteers to perform their dialogues for the class.

GRAMMAR AND EXPRESSIONS:
Apologizing, Making Excuses, Accepting an Apology

Apologizing	Making Excuses	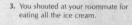 Accepting an Apology
When you are sorry for bothering or possibly for making a problem for someone, you *apologize*.	After you apologize, you often try to explain by *making excuses*.	After someone apologizes to *you*, you might say something kind to *accept the apology*.
Harry arrives late to Susan's apartment. To apologize, he says, "Sorry I'm late."	Harry makes excuses for being late: To make excuses, he says, "The traffic. The parking. I was lost."	Susan accepts Harry's apology by saying, "Don't worry about being late. It's fine."
Susan apologizes because her apartment is not in order: She says, "Excuse the mess."	Susan makes an excuse for her messy apartment: She says, "I just moved here."	Because Harry was nervous, he didn't say anything to accept Susan's apology. In this situation, someone might say, "It looks like a nice place" *or* "My place is much more messy."

IN PAIRS

With a partner, play each of the following situations. In each situation, *apologize* and also *make an excuse*. Your partner will *accept your apology* to make you feel better. You can choose other expressions for apologizing from the Conversation Box.

1. You forgot your mother's birthday.

2. You spilled coffee on your friend's carpet.

3. You shouted at your roommate for eating all the ice cream.

CONVERSATION BOX
- Please forgive me for (+ *-ing* verb)
- I'm so sorry for (+ *-ing* verb)

USEFUL LANGUAGE

In Act I, you heard ways to . . .

- ask for help:
  Excuse me. Can you help me?
- say good-bye to someone you just met:
  Hope to see you again.
- apologize:
  Sorry I'm . . .
  Excuse the mess.

- ask for directions:
  Where is . . .?
  I'm looking for . . .
- give directions:
  Make a left turn. Then walk two blocks to the traffic light.
- make excuses:
  I was lost.
  I just moved here.

- accept an apology:
  Don't worry about . . .
  It's fine.
- say a telephone number so someone can reach you:
  I'll be at 555-1720.
- accept a gift:
  What pretty flowers!

IN PAIRS

↕

INSTANT ROLE-PLAYS

Practice this conversation with a partner:

On the street . . .

A: Excuse me. I'm new here. Where is the nearest subway station?

B: That's easy. Go three blocks and make a left.

A: Three blocks and a left?

B: That's right. The station will be on your right.

A: On the right. Thanks. I appreciate your help.

B: No problem.

Then complete this conversation:

In the school cafeteria . . .

A: Excuse me. I'm new here. Where are the rest rooms?

B:

A:

B:

A:

B:

READ AND DISCUSS

Read the paragraphs under "U.S. Life." Then discuss your answers to the questions under "Your Turn."

ON YOUR OWN

U.S. LIFE

Most Americans are happy to give directions on the street. When Harry asked for directions, he started with, *Excuse me.* This is the usual way to begin a conversation with a stranger or to ask for information.

When asking for directions, it often helps to add a little explanation, such as *I'm new here* or *I'm afraid I'm lost.* You can also start with a question, such as *Do you know this area?* Or *Can you tell me how to get to . . .?*

Always repeat the directions after you hear them. Repeating will help you remember, and it shows the person helping you that you understand.

IN SMALL GROUPS

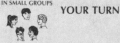

YOUR TURN

1. Do you feel comfortable with asking strangers for directions?
2. Do you have experience with asking for directions in a strange city?
3. Do people often ask you for directions?
4. Did you ever give the wrong directions to a place?

USEFUL LANGUAGE

PREPARE

With the students, read through the expressions in the box.

PARTICIPATE

1. Have students close their books.
2. Give each cue below. Elicit appropriate responses from the class. The possible student answers are in parentheses.

Teacher:	What's your home telephone number?
Student:	(Answers will vary.)
Teacher:	Well, I have to go now.
Student:	(Hope to see you again.)
Teacher:	How do I get to the library?
Student:	(Answers will vary.)
Teacher:	Why are you so late to class today?
Student:	(Excuses will vary.)
Teacher:	I'm sorry I lost your book.
Student:	(Don't worry about it. *or* It's fine.)
Teacher:	Here. I brought these roses for you.
Student:	(What pretty roses!)

INSTANT ROLE-PLAYS

On the street . . .

PARTICIPATE

1. Practice the dialogue with the class by taking part A yourself and allowing the class to play part B together.
2. Exchange parts. Have students say part A together.
3. Have students practice the dialogue with their partner.

In the school cafeteria . . .

PARTICIPATE

1. Have students create a dialogue with their partner.
2. Select student pairs to perform for the class.

U.S. LIFE

PARTICIPATE

1. Have students read independently.
2. Ask for volunteers to read the passage aloud.

YOUR TURN

Have students discuss their answers to the questions in small groups or with the entire class.

LESSON TWO
ACT II PREVIEW

PREPARE

1. Pre-teach: *Thailand, Thai food.*
2. If you have a multi-national class, elicit from your students the names of the countries they come from and the corresponding adjectives. (Examples: *Spain, Spanish; the Philippines, Filipino.*) If your class is a single nationality, elicit the names of countries they have visited with the corresponding adjective forms.

PARTICIPATE

1. With the class, read the instructions and the dialogue beneath each photo.
2. Turn the sound off and play the Preview (31:55 to 32:39).
3. Have students circle their choices.
4. Turn the sound on and replay the Preview to discover the correct answers.

EXTEND

Elicit possible answers to the question: *Why is Harry leaving?* Tell students they will find out in Act II.

LOOK WHO'S TALKING

PREPARE

Pre-teach: *welcome, special, ginger ale, dry white wine, chablis* (pronounced: *sha-blee*), *crispy, noodles, recommend, rose-petal salad.*

PARTICIPATE

1. With the class, read the instructions.
2. Play the scene (32:40 to 34:22).
3. Have students complete the exercise on their own.
4. Review the correct answers.

_____
ACT II
PREVIEW

SOUND OFF

31:55 - 32:39

With the sound off, watch the preview. Look for the two scenes in the pictures below. What are the people saying? Circle *a, b,* or *c.*

Somsak:
a. What would you like to eat?
b. Would you like something to eat?
c. Are you hungry tonight?

Harry:
a. I'll have the mee krob also.
b. I'm hungry, too.
c. I like your restaurant.

Now, **with the sound on,** watch the preview again to check your answers.

_____
ACT II
VIDEO GAMES

Scene 1: "Follow me, please."

LOOK WHO'S TALKING

SOUND ON

32:40 - 34:22

Watch the scene and listen to it carefully. Who said each of the following sentences? Write *Harry, Susan,* or *Somsak* on each blank line. The first answer is given.

1. **Somsak:** Any friend of Miss Stewart's is welcome at Somsak's.
2. _____ : I like it here
3. _____ : A special place for special people.
4. _____ : Would you like something to drink?
5. _____ : I'd like a glass of ginger ale with ice.
6. _____ : Do you have a dry white wine?
7. _____ : How about a California chablis?
8. _____ : Harry, would you like to see a menu?
9. _____ : I'll have the mee krob also.
10. _____ : What is it?
11. _____ : I recommend rose-petal salad.
12. _____ : I'll take care of everything.
13. _____ : I hope you're hungry.

Scene 2: "Here we are."

LISTEN IN

SOUND ON

34:23 - 35:48

Read the statements below. Then watch the scene and listen to it carefully. Which of the following items are true according to the information in the scene? Put a check (✔) in the box **only if you are sure the sentence is true**.

- ☐ **1.** Harry is older than Susan.
- ☐ **2.** Harry is an accountant.
- ☐ **3.** Harry is hungry.
- ☐ **4.** Susan is a vice-president of a toy company.
- ☐ **5.** Susan works six days a week.
- ☐ **6.** Susan develops new toys.
- ☐ **7.** Harry's daughter is nine years old.
- ☐ **8.** Harry likes his job.
- ☐ **9.** Harry lives in the suburbs.

BEHIND THE SCENES

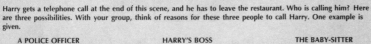

IN SMALL GROUPS

Harry gets a telephone call at the end of this scene, and he has to leave the restaurant. Who is calling him? Here are three possibilities. With your group, think of reasons for these three people to call Harry. One example is given.

A POLICE OFFICER	HARRY'S BOSS	THE BABY-SITTER

- Maybe someone stole Harry's car.
- Maybe . . .

- Maybe . . .
- Maybe . . .

- Maybe . . .
- Maybe . . .

LISTEN IN

PREPARE
Pre-teach: *hungry, starving, toy, company* (business), *vice-president, development, terrific, accountant, CPA (certified public accountant)*

PARTICIPATE
1. With the class, read the instructions and the statements 1–9 below.
2. Play the scene (34:23 to 35:48).
3. Have students complete the exercise on their own.
4. Replay the scene to check the answers.

BEHIND THE SCENES

PARTICIPATE
1. With the class, read the instructions.
2. Have the class work in small groups. Have each group think of at least two possible reasons for each of the three people to call Harry. Students may write their answers if they wish.
3. Elicit answers from the groups. Select and standardize the responses.

SPLIT DIALOGUE

PREPARE

Pre-teach: *forgive, terrible, feel well, serious, stomachache, cry, sorry, chance* (opportunity), *another, worry, all right, What's the matter?*

PARTICIPATE

1. With the class, read the instructions.
2. Play the scene (35:49 to 36:36).
3. Have the students work in pairs to complete the exercise. (More advanced students will be able to complete the dialogue for both Susan and Harry.)
4. Replay the scene to check the answers.

FURTHER PRACTICE

Have students practice reading the dialogue with their partner.

EXTEND

1. Have students extend the scene. Tell them to imagine that Somsak comes back to Susan's table after Harry leaves. He asks what happened. Susan explains about Harry's daughter. Write the dialogue with your partner.
2. Ask for volunteers to perform their new scene for the class.

FOCUS IN: OFFERING AND ORDERING

PREPARE

Pre-teach: *herbal tea, dessert.*

PARTICIPATE

1. With the class, read the instructions.
2. Play the "Focus In" segment (36:37 to 38:50).
3. Replay the segment and encourage students to sing along.

Scene 3: *"Please forgive me."*

SPLIT DIALOGUE

IN PAIRS

SOUND ON
35:49 - 36:36

Watch the scene to complete the sentences below. Work with a partner. One of you will complete Harry's lines; the other will complete Susan's. Choose the correct words from the Word Box. Two answers are given. Play the scene as many times as necessary.

Harry

1. Please **forgive** me, Susan, but . . . I have to leave. I _____ terrible, but . . .
2. My _____ isn't feeling well.
3. I don't know. The _____ says she has a stomachache, and she's crying. I'll have to go _____. Will you forgive me?
4. Oh, it's OK. Let me _____ you home first.
5. It's our first _____.
6. I'll _____ you.
7. Good-bye.

WORD BOX

worry
date
serious
feel
phone
Please
sorry
baby-sitter
forgive
chance
home
all right
take
matter
daughter

Susan

1. What's the **matter**?
2. Oh no! Is it _____?
3. Of course. I'm so _____ for Michelle. And you didn't have a _____ to eat.
4. No, no. _____, go ahead.
5. We'll make another. Please don't _____.
6. I hope your daughter is _____. Good-bye.

Now watch the scene again. Check your answers with your partner. Then practice reading the dialogue together.

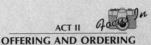

ACT II
OFFERING AND ORDERING

WITH THE WHOLE CLASS

SOUND ON
36:37 - 38:50

Watch the "Focus In" segment. Then watch it again and sing along.

ACT II
INTERMISSION
GRAMMAR AND EXPRESSIONS: At a Restaurant

When they ordered their food, Susan said, *"I'd like the mee krob."* Harry said, *"I'll have the mee krob also."*

I'd like (+noun phrase or infinitive phrase)

Use *I'd like* (+noun phrase) to order food or drinks:

- *I'd like a hamburger.*
- *I'd like a cup of coffee.*

You may also use *I'd like* (+infinitive phrase):

- *I'd like to try a new dish.*
- *I'd like to begin with a salad.*

I'll (+simple verb)

Use *I'll* (+simple verb) to order food or drinks:

- *I'll have a tuna salad sandwich.*
- *I'll try your special salad.*
- *I'll take the soup of the day.*
- *I'll begin with a glass of white wine.*

IN PAIRS

Use the menu below to practice ordering in a restaurant. Work with a partner. One of you will play the waiter; the other will be the customer. Then change parts. Use expressions from the Conversation Box to offer and order.

Soup
HOMEMADE DELICIOUS SOUP Cup 1.45 Bowl 1.85

Entrees
ROAST FRESH TURKEY with Cranberry
  Sauce, Vegetable, Potato & Salad 9.75
CHOPPED SIRLOIN STEAK with Potato,
  Vegetable & Salad 8.50
HAM STEAK with Pineapple Rings, Potato,
  Vegetable & Salad 9.75
LIVER & ONION with Potato,
  Vegetable & Salad 8.25
BROILED SHRIMP with Rice,
  Vegetable & Salad 9.75
BROILED HALIBUT with Rice,
  Vegetable & Salad 9.75
VEAL CUTLET with Potato,
  Vegetable & Salad 10.25
CHICKEN CUTLET with Potato,
  Vegetable & Salad 9.25
1/2 BROILED CHICKEN with Potato,
  Vegetable & Salad 8.90
LAMB CHOPS (3) with Mint Jelly, Vegetables,
  Potato & Salad 15.75
PORK CHOPS (2) with Apple Sauce, Potato,
  Vegetable & Salad 10.25
SIRLOIN STEAK with Potato,
  Vegetable & Salad 16.25

Desserts
HOMEMADE FRUIT PIES
  (apple, cherry, or blueberry) 1.25
  with whipped cream 1.55
POUND CAKE .1.00
LAYER CAKE 1.45
PLAIN CHEESECAKE 1.95
RICE PUDDING (homemade) 1.25
ICE CREAM
  (vanilla, chocolate, or strawberry) 1.95

Beverages
COFFEE 60   MILK 75
TEA 60   CHOCOLATE MILK . .95
BREWED DECAF . . .70   HOT CHOCOLATE . . .75
ICED TEA 95   BEER 1.95
ICED COFFEE 95   GLASS OF WINE . 1.75
SOFT DRINKS 1.25

CONVERSATION BOX

Waiter

- What would you like to eat?
- Would you like (a salad)?
- Would you like something to drink?
- How about . . . ?
- May I recommend . . . ?

Customer

- I'll have . . .
- I'll begin with . . .
- I'd like . . .
- I'll try . . .
- What do you recommend?

ACT II INTERMISSION
GRAMMAR AND EXPRESSIONS
AT A RESTAURANT

PREPARE

1. With the class, read through the examples of the uses of *I'd like . . .* and *I'll . . . .*
2. Conduct a substitution drill:

   Teacher: Repeat: I'd like a cup of coffee.
   Student: I'd like a cup of coffee.
   Teacher: Change my sentence. Use *have*:
   Student: I'll have a cup of coffee.
   Teacher: *hamburger*
   Student. I'll have a hamburger.
   Teacher: like
   Student: I'd like a hamburger.
   Teacher: try
   Student: I'll try a hamburger.
   (other substitutions: *glass of wine, take, like, begin with*)

PARTICIPATE

1. With the class, read the instructions.
2. Have students work in pairs to complete the role-play activity. If students have brought menus from their favorite restaurants, they may use these instead of the menu provided in the book.
3. Encourage students to perform their dialogue for the class.

USEFUL LANGUAGE

PREPARE

With the students, read through the expressions in the box.

PARTICIPATE

1. Have students close their books.
2. Give each cue below. Elicit appropriate responses from the class. The possible student answers are in parentheses.

Teacher: What should we order for dinner?
Student: (I recommend_____ or How about_____.)
Teacher: My mother is sick.
Student: (What's the matter with her? or Is it serious?)
Teacher: My brother has a wonderful job.
Student: (What does he do?)
Teacher: I'm sorry that you're leaving so early.
Student: (Please forgive me.)

INSTANT ROLE-PLAYS

At a party . . .

PARTICIPATE

1. Practice the dialogue with the class by taking part A yourself and allowing the class to play part B together.
2. Exchange parts. Have students say part A together.
3. Have students practice the dialogue with their partner.

At a class reunion . . .

PARTICIPATE

1. Have students create a dialogue with their partner.
2. Select student pairs to perform for the class.

On the street . . .

PARTICIPATE

1. Practice the dialogue with the class by taking part A yourself and allowing the class to play part B together.
2. Exchange parts. Have students say part A together.
3. Have students practice the dialogue with their partner.

At the restaurant, as the waiter brings the check . . .

PARTICIPATE

1. Have students create a dialogue with their partner.
2. Select student pairs to perform for the class.

LESSON THREE
ACT III PREVIEW

PREPARE

1. Pre-teach: *delicious, What does he/she/it mean?*
2. Review: *apologize.*

PARTICIPATE

1. Play the Preview (38:55 to 39:35).
2. With the class, read the instructions and the question below each photo.
3. Elicit answers to question 1 from the class.
   Teacher: Did Susan stay at the restaurant and eat alone?
   What did she decide to do?
   Elicit answers to questions 2 and 3.
4. Replay the Preview if necessary.
5. Review the correct answers.

USEFUL LANGUAGE

In Act II, you heard ways to . . .

- order something to eat or drink:
  I'd like the mee krob.
  I'll have the mee krob.
  Do you have a dry white wine?
- make a suggestion:
  How about . . .?
  I recommend . . .

- greet someone:
  Welcome!
- ask about someone's job:
  What do you do?
- excuse yourself:
  Please forgive me.

- ask about a problem:
  What's the matter?
  Is it serious?
- express concern:
  I hope nothing is wrong.
  I hope your daughter is all right.

IN PAIRS

↕

INSTANT ROLE-PLAYS

Practice these conversations with a partner:

At a party . . .

A. Where do you work?
B. I work at the Bay Company.
A. What do you do there?
B. I'm a supervisor.

During the movie . . .

A. I'm sorry. I have to go.
B. What's the matter?
A. I'm not feeling very well.
B. I hope it's not serious.
A. Please forgive me. We didn't see the end of the movie.
B. Don't worry. We'll see it another time.

Then complete these conversations:

At a class reunion . . .

A. Hi, _____. What do you do now?
B.
A.
B.

At the restaurant, as the waiter brings the check . . .

A. Oh no, I left my wallet at home!
B.
A.
B.

ACT III
PREVIEW

SOUND ON

38:55 - 39:35

Watch the preview. Then guess the answers to the following questions.

1. What kind of food are Susan and Marilyn eating?

2. Why is Harry bringing something to Susan?

3. Susan asks Harry, "Is there anyone else in your life?" What does she mean?

ACT III PREVIEW (*continued*)

EXTEND

Elicit possible answers to the question: *Will Susan and Harry see each other again?* (Hint: What does Harry mean when he says, "Not yet"?)

ACT III
VIDEO GAMES

Scene 1: "You won't believe it, Marilyn!"

TABLE TALK

SOUND ON
39:36 - 41:10

Use the expressions from the Phrase Box to write the missing questions in Susan and Marilyn's conversation. Then watch the scene to check your answers.

Marilyn: (1) _____
Susan: The baby-sitter called. His daughter is sick.

Marilyn: (2) _____
Susan: I think she has a stomachache. He's a good father.

Marilyn: (3) _____
Susan: He's very nice. But I think he was nervous tonight. It was his first date in two years.

Marilyn: (4) _____
Susan: I hope so.

PHRASE BOX

What's wrong?
So . . . what do you think of him?
What happened?
Will you see him again?

WITH THE WHOLE CLASS

FREEZE!

PAUSE AT 41:10

Why did Harry come back? Discuss your opinions. You will find out the answer in the next scene!

TABLE TALK

PREPARE
1. Pre-teach: *nervous*.
2. Read aloud the questions in the Phrase Box and have students repeat them.

PARTICIPATE
1. With the class, read the instructions.
2. Have students complete the exercise on their own.
3. Play the scene (39:36 to 41:10).
4. Review the correct answers.

FREEZE!
1. Replay the scene and pause at 41:10.
2. Invite class discussion about these questions:
   Why did Harry come back?
   Is his daughter seriously ill?
   Why is he holding a plant?

LISTEN IN

PREPARE

Pre-teach: *downstairs neighbor, bonsai tree, join, agree, as a matter of fact, enjoy, fashion show, close* (adjective, as in *close friends*).

PARTICIPATE

1. With the class, read the instructions and statements 1–9.
2. Play the scene (41:11 to 42:42).
3. Have students complete the exercise on their own.
4. Replay the scene to check the answers.

THE SUBTEXT

PREPARE

1. Pre-teach: *miss* (a person), *occasionally, speaking of . . . , midnight, too, promise, safe trip, umbrella stand.*
2. To introduce students to the idea of a *subtext*, role-play both parts in these examples:

   a. A husband comes home from work. His wife is crying.

   Wife: Honey, I lost my ring. I feel terrible.

   Husband: Well . . . Now we can buy a better one.

   What is the husband really saying? He's saying, "Don't be upset. It's only a ring." This is the *subtext*.

   b. An employee is late for work three times in one week. He makes an excuse to his boss.

   Employee: I'm sorry I'm late again. But I live so far from here.

   Boss: I know. I think tomorrow you should look for a job near your home.

   What is the boss really saying? He's saying, "You're fired." In other words, "You can't keep this job, anymore." This is the *subtext*.

PARTICIPATE

1. With the class, read the thoughts in the two balloons and the instructions below.
2. Play the scene (42:43 to 44:41). Students may tell you to pause in several different places. When a student tells you to pause, ask the student to repeat what Susan or Harry said.

Scene 2: "I hope it's not too late."

LISTEN IN

SOUND ON

41:11 - 42:42

Read the statements below. Then watch the scene and listen to it carefully. Which of the following items are true according to the information in the scene? Put a check (✔) in the box only if you are sure the sentence is true.

☐ 1. A neighbor let Harry into Susan's building.

☐ 2. Harry's daughter is feeling better.

☐ 3. Harry bought the bonsai tree at a discount store.

☐ 4. Susan knew Harry would come back.

☐ 5. Harry's daughter doesn't like him to go on dates.

☐ 6. Marilyn is tired from working all day.

☐ 7. Marilyn is going to a fashion show tomorrow.

☐ 8. Marilyn is sleeping at Susan's apartment tonight.

☐ 9. Susan and Harry made a date to see each other next week.

Scene 3: "Oh, I date occasionally."

WITH THE WHOLE CLASS

THE SUBTEXT

SOUND ON

42:43 - 44:41

Do you have a special woman in your life? I hope not because I like you.

I'm having such a good time with you. I don't want to leave.

Read Susan's and Harry's thoughts above. Then watch the scene and listen to their conversation. What do Susan and Harry say to express these feelings? Tell your teacher to stop the tape when you hear each answer.

ACT III
OCCUPATIONS

SOUND ON

44:42 - 46:30

Watch the "Focus In" segment. Then watch it again and sing along. The pictures will help you follow the words to the song.

He's an accountant.
He works with numbers.
He's an accountant.
He manages your money.
He's an accountant.
He plans your taxes.
An accountant—
That's his occupation,
His job.

She's in business.
She's a vice-president—
A vice-president
In a toy company.
She's in business.
She's the boss.
A vice-president—
That's her occupation,
Her job.

She's a salesclerk.
She sells clothing.
She's a salesclerk.
She works in a store.
Yeah, she's a salesclerk.
She designs clothing, too.
A salesclerk—
That's her occupation,
Her job.

She's a teacher.
That's her job.

She's a nurse.
That's her job.

He's a pilot.
That's his job.

Those are occupations. They're all jobs.
_____ _____ _____. That's her job.
_____ _____ _____. That's her job.
_____ _____ _____. That's his job.
Those are occupations. They're all jobs.

He's a vendor.
He sells food
On the street.
He's a vendor.
He sells hot
dogs.
Yeah!
He's a vendor.
He sells ice
cream.
A vendor,
An accountant,
A salesclerk,
A nurse,
A teacher,
A pilot—
They're all jobs!

FOCUS IN: OCCUPATIONS

PREPARE
Pre-teach: *accountant, manage money, taxes, business, salesclerk, clothing, to design, nurse, pilot, vendor.*

PARTICIPATE
1. With the class, read the instructions.
2. Play the "Focus In" segment (44:42 to 46:30).
3. Replay the segment and encourage students to sing along.
4. Note that a male voice alternates with a female voice in the song. Divide your class into two groups and assign a part to each.
5. Replay the segment and have students sing along.

ACT III FINALE
BEHIND THE SCENES

PREPARE

1. Pre-teach the affirmative and negative short answers *I think so* and *I don't think so*. Elicit one of these short answers by asking the following questions:
   a. Are you a good student?
   b. Is English a difficult language?
   c. Will we finish watching this episode today?
   d. Do you understand this lesson?

2. Pre-teach the affirmative and negative short answers *I hope so* and *I hope not*. Elicit one of these short answers by asking the following questions:
   a. Will you speak good English soon?
   b. Is it going to rain today?
   c. Is your boss going to fire you?
   d. Are you going to visit (the United States/your native country) soon?

3. Repeat the questions from 1 and 2 above. Encourage students to give a reason for each of their answers.

PARTICIPATE

1. With the class, read the instructions.
2. Have students work in small groups to complete the exercise. Circulate among the groups to assist the students.
3. Elicit answers from the whole class.

PRONUNCIATON

PARTICIPATE

1. With the class, read the explanation and the instructions.
2. Have the students complete the exercise.
3. Review the correct answers. Have students read each sentence aloud.

DATING SERVICE

1. With the class, read the instructions.
2. Have students work in pairs to complete the activity. Be sure that students exchange roles.

EXTEND

Have each student write a paragraph about himself or herself—similar to Harry's paragraph. Each student should write the paragraphs on a separate piece of paper, which you will collect for the TELEPLAYS activity on the next page.

IN SMALL GROUPS

ACT III
FINALE
BEHIND THE SCENES

Answer these questions with your group. Tell your opinions and give a reason for each answer. Use one of the expressions from the Conversation Box to begin each answer. Some possible answers are given.

1. Will Harry call Susan soon?
   I hope so. They make a nice couple. • *I don't think so. He's too shy.*
2. Does Susan have time to cook?
   I don't think so. She eats at restaurants a lot.
3. Does Harry come from a large family?
4. Will Harry remember how to get to Susan's apartment?
5. Does Susan like children?
6. Would Harry like a new relationship in his life? Would Susan?
7. Will Susan call Harry if he is too shy to call her?

CONVERSATION BOX
I think so.
I hope so.
I don't think so.
I hope not.

PRONUNCIATION

Harry says, "I think we're *going to* be good friends." His informal pronunciation is "I think we're *gonna* be good friends." When *going to* is a future auxiliary, you often hear *gonna*. But when *going to* is a main verb with a preposition, you don't hear the *gonna* pronunciation. For example, in the sentence, "I'm *going to* the store," you never hear *gonna* because *going* is a main verb and *to* is a preposition.

You might hear *gonna* in only *two* of the following sentences. Underline those two sentences.

1. I'm going to your house.
2. When are you going to call me?
3. Are you going to the movies tonight?
4. We're going to have a good time.

IN PAIRS

DATING SERVICE

A *dating service* introduces single people to each other. People give this type of company personal information. The dating service tries to match *singles* who might be *compatible*, who might become good friends because they have the same interests.

Read Harry's Personal Data Form. Then read the way he tells this information at an interview at a dating service. Complete the blank Personal Data Form below. Then your partner will interview you to help you find a date.

PERSONAL DATA FORM	
Name:	*Harry Bennett*
Age:	*33*
Height:	*5'10"*
Occupation:	*Certified Public Accountant*
Hobbies:	*reading mystery novels foreign travel tennis*

"Hi, I'm Harry Bennett. I'm 33 and about average height. I'm an accountant. I love numbers. My favorite activities are reading mysteries, visiting faraway places, and playing tennis."

PERSONAL DATA FORM
Name:
Age:
Height:
Occupation:
Hobbies:

USEFUL LANGUAGE

In Act III, you heard ways to . . .

- ask about a past event:
  What happened?.
- ask about a problem:
  What's wrong?
- express surprise:
  You won't believe it!
- leave someone after a date:
  I had a nice evening.
- excuse yourself for making a surprise visit at a late hour:
  I hope it's not too late.

- accept an excuse:
  Not at all.
- invite someone to enter:
  Come in. Join us.
- make a promise:
  I promise I won't leave early.
- leave a group of people:
  I'm going to excuse myself.
- ask if someone has another relationship right now:
  Is there anyone else in your life?

- introduce a new idea in a conversation:
  Speaking of . . .
  You know something?
- wish someone a safe trip:
  Have a safe trip home.

IN PAIRS

INSTANT ROLE-PLAYS

Practice these conversations with a partner:

During a meeting . . .

A. I'm going to excuse myself. I have a plane to catch.
B. Where can we reach you?
A. I'll be at (213) 555-2367. You can reach me there.
B. Have a safe trip.

Then complete these conversations:

At the office . . .

A. You won't believe it!
B.
A.
B.

At a neighbor's house at 10 P.M. . . .

A. I hope it's not too late.
B. Not at all. Can I help you?
A. The lights are out in my apartment. I need to borrow a flashlight.
B. Here you are.
A. Thanks. I'll bring it right back.
B. Don't worry. Bring it back tomorrow.

At a neighbor's house at 7 A.M. . . .

A. I hope it's not too early.
B.
A.
B.
A.
B.

IN SMALL GROUPS

TELEPLAYS

A. Imagine that you want to arrange a date between two of your friends or two people in your class. What would you tell each one about the other?
B. Be TV writers. Write a script about the date between the two people in Part A. What happened when they went out together?

TELEPLAYS (continued)

4. Have the groups read the paragraphs to choose two students that seem to be a good match.
5. Have students write a dialogue that occurs during an imaginary blind date between this couple. (Students may also choose to write the story of the date in paragraph form.) Circulate among the groups and encourage students to make comments that are positive and in good taste about their couple. Each group may work together to write about one couple. Or pairs of students may choose different couples to write about.
6. Select examples to read to the class.

USEFUL LANGUAGE

PREPARE
With the students, read through the expressions in the box.

PARTICIPATE
1. Have students close their books.
2. Give each cue below. Elicit appropriate expressions from the class for each situation. The possible student answers are in parentheses.

Teacher: I'm glad you invited me to go out with you.
Student: (I had a nice evening.)
Teacher: You were late to class today.
Student: (I promise I won't be late again.)
Teacher: Oh, I see you have guests. I'll come back tomorrow.
Student: (Come in. Join us.)
Teacher: Oh, no!
Student: (What happened *or* What's wrong?)
Teacher: Bye-bye.
Student: (Have a safe trip home.)
Teacher: Come in. I'm not sleeping yet.
Student: (I hope it's not too late.)

INSTANT ROLE-PLAYS

During a meeting . . .
PARTICIPATE
1. Practice the dialogue with the class by taking part A yourself and allowing the class to play part B together.
2. Exchange parts. Have students say part A together.
3. Have students practice the dialogue with their partner.

At the office . . .
PARTICIPATE
1. Have students create a dialogue with their partner.
2. Select student pairs to perform for the class.

At a neighbor's house at 10 P.M. . . .
PARTICIPATE
1. Practice the dialogue with the class by taking part A yourself and allowing the class to play part B together.
2. Exchange parts. Have students say part A together.
3. Have students practice the dialogue with their partner.

At a neighbor's house at 7 A.M. . . .
PARTICIPATE
1. Have students create a dialogue with their partner.
2. Select student pairs to perform for the class.

TELEPLAYS

PREPARE
Note: This activity asks students to talk in personal terms about their classmates or friends. You may wish to revise the activity so that groups write about imaginary people.

PARTICIPATE
1. With the class, read the instructions for A and B.
2. Divide the class into small groups.
3. Collect the paragraphs students wrote about themselves for the DATING SERVICE (EXTEND) activity on page 30. Redistribute the papers to other groups.

U.S. LIFE

PREPARE

Pre-teach: *unusual, to have something in common, to share, to arrange.*

PARTICIPATE

1. Have students read independently.
2. Read each of the following statements to the class. Ask students to say whether the statement is true or false. The answers are given in parentheses.
   a. Harry met Susan at a church group. (*False.*)
   b. All Americans like blind dates. (*False.*)
   c. Blind dates are usually arranged by family members or friends. (*True.*)

YOUR TURN

Have students discuss their answers to the questions in small groups or with the entire class.

STORYWRITER

1. With the class, read the instructions.
2. Have students choose which of the subjects they wish to write about.
3. Give students ten minutes to write.
4. Have students exchange papers. Ask for volunteers to stand up and read their classmate's paper aloud.

READ AND DISCUSS

Read the paragraphs under "U.S. Life." Then discuss your answers to the questions under "Your Turn."

ON YOUR OWN

U.S. LIFE

Harry and Susan went on a **blind date.** They didn't know each other before. Blind dates are common in the United States. A family member or friend may know a man and a woman who *have a lot in common*—who share the same interests or background. So the friend or family member will arrange a blind date for the man and woman to meet.

Some people enjoy blind dates very much. They like meeting and finding out about someone new. Other people get very nervous at the idea of meeting and spending time with someone they don't know.

Single people can also meet each other through clubs and organizations, such as church or political groups, or through dating services.

IN SMALL GROUPS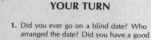

YOUR TURN

1. Did you ever go on a blind date? Who arranged the date? Did you have a good time?
2. Do you enjoy matching single men with single women?
3. Do you prefer to be with a person similar to yourself? Or do you believe that "opposites attract"?

ON YOUR OWN

STORYWRITER

By yourself, write about one of the following:

- Write the story of this episode for someone who didn't see it.
- Describe one of the characters in this episode. How is this person similar to you—but also different from you?
- Write about your first date with someone.

EPISODE 3: "Grandpa's Trunk"

EPISODE 3

"Grandpa's Trunk"

In this unit, you will practice . . .

giving your opinion
giving personal information
talking about your family

ACT I

SOUND ON
1:00 - 1:40

Read these questions. Then watch the preview to find the answers. Write the answers on the blank lines.

1. Why are the Stewarts excited? _____
2. In which part of the house will Grandpa stay? _____
3. Why are Ellen and Marilyn planning to go upstairs? _____
4. What is Richard going to give Grandpa? _____
5. Why does Philip come into Grandpa's room? _____

ACT I
VIDEO GAMES

Scene 1: "I am so excited!"

THE RIGHT ORDER

SOUND ON
1:41 - 2:59

IN PAIRS

Watch the scene between Marilyn and Ellen. Work with a partner to say this dialogue in the right order.

MARILYN	ELLEN
—Are we picking him up at the station?	—I am so excited! At this time tomorrow morning, Grandpa will be sitting in the kitchen with us.
—When does he arrive?	—Not Grandpa. He doesn't want anybody picking him up. He likes to be independent.
—Coffee, please.	—Marilyn, you want coffee or tea?
—Huh.	—Oh, let's go upstairs and prepare Grandpa's room.
—Great! Let's do it!	—At six o'clock this evening.
—By plane?	—No, by train.

"Grandpa's Trunk" ● 33

THE RIGHT ORDER (continued)
3. Have students work in pairs to say the dialogue in the correct order.
4. Play the scene again to review the correct sequence.
5. Ask for volunteers to read the dialogue aloud.

EPISODE 3: "Grandpa's Trunk"

SUMMARY
Malcolm Stewart arrives by train from Florida to live with his son Philip's family.

LANGUAGE
• giving your opinion
• talking about future schedules (simple present tense)
• giving personal information
• talking about your family

U.S. LIFE
• retirement
• senior citizens
• extended families

ADVANCE PLANNING
1. Ask students to bring to class a photo that shows a special personal memory. They will need the photos for an activity on page 45.
2. Tell students to research two or three generations of their family history. They will use the information (to make a family tree) in an activity on page 47.

LESSON ONE
ACT I PREVIEW
PREPARE
Pre-teach: *arrival, welcome present, hangers, trunk.*

PARTICIPATE
1. With the class, read the instructions and questions 1–5.
2. Have students watch the entire Preview (1:00 to 1:40) without writing.
3. Have students work in pairs (Student A and Student B). Have Student A ask Student B questions 1–3, and Student B ask Student A questions 4–5.
4. Play the Preview again so students can check their answers.

EXTEND
Elicit possible answers to the question: *What's inside the trunk?* (Hint: Grandpa is very proud of his family.)

THE RIGHT ORDER
PREPARE
1. Pre-teach: *excited, by plane, by train, by car, on foot, to pick up someone* (to go by car to meet someone and give the person a ride), *independent, fella* (informal for "fellow"), *to set up* (to prepare).
2. Pre-teach the future progressive verb tense:
   a. On the board, write tomorrow's date and 7 P.M.
   b. Tell students to close their eyes and imagine that the time is tomorrow evening at 7 P.M. Ask, "What will you be doing?" Elicit the activities with the structure *I will be____-ing . . . .*
   c. Have students ask each other and answer the question about other specified future times (e.g., at three o'clock next Saturday, at six o'clock tomorrow morning).

PARTICIPATE
1. With the class, read the instructions.
2. Play the scene (1:41 to 2:59).

WHO DOES IT?

PREPARE

1. Pre-teach: *funny, fun, to laugh, comfortable, crazy, that's for sure, to put together, neat* (good, great), *He's something!* (to express admiration), *junior high school, graduation*.
2. CULTURE NOTE: Robbie refers to the "Fathers and Sons' Breakfast" at his junior high school graduation. Explain to your students that events and holidays sometimes begin with a public breakfast ceremony.
3. Write these verbs on the board: *get, bring, put, pour, open, drink, show*. Mime the meaning of each verb. Ask students to identify the correct verb for each action.

PARTICIPATE

1. With the class, read the instructions.
2. Turn the sound off and play the scene (3:00 to 4:02).
3. Have students complete the exercise.
4. Play the scene again to review the correct answers.

FURTHER PRACTICE

1. Put several objects on a desk or table in the front of the room. Ask for a student volunteer.
2. Have students use the verbs on the board to give commands to the volunteer.

WHO SAYS IT?

PARTICIPATE

1. With the class, read the instructions.
2. Turn the sound on and play the scene (3:00 to 4:02).
3. Have students complete the exercise.
4. Replay the scene to check the answers.

Scene 2: "That's a neat idea."

WHO DOES IT?

SOUND OFF

3:00 - 4:02

With the sound off, watch the scene. Who does each of the following actions? Write *Robbie* or *Richard* on the line at the beginning of each sentence. The first answer is given.

1. *Robbie* gets the cereal from the cabinet.
2. _____ brings the cereal bowls to the table.
3. _____ asks for the milk.
4. _____ puts the spoons on the table.

5. _____ pours the orange juice.
6. _____ opens the cereal box.
7. _____ drinks some orange juice.
8. _____ shows a picture.

WHO SAYS IT?

SOUND ON

3:00 - 4:02

Now, with the sound on, watch the scene again. Listen to Robbie and Richard's conversation. Read each of the statements or questions below. Who says each one? Write *Robbie* or *Richard* in the space before each item. Then circle *a* or *b* to show Robbie's or Richard's meaning. The first answer is given.

1. *Robbie* : I'm really excited about seeing Grandpa.
   a. I'm very happy that Grandpa is coming.
   b. I'm angry that Grandpa is coming to live here.

2. _____ : He always makes me laugh.
   a. Grandpa is a happy man.
   b. Grandpa tells a lot of jokes.

3. _____ : It just takes time to feel comfortable in a new place.
   a. Grandpa will not have any problems when he comes to live with the Stewarts.
   b. Sometimes people are unhappy for a few weeks or months in a new city or house.

4. _____ : Won't he miss being in Florida?
   a. Maybe he will be sorry that he left Florida.
   b. Maybe he will like New York better than Florida.

5. _____ : It's crazy here most of the time.
   a. The family members are very busy, and they come and go at different times of the day.
   b. The family members are very noisy, and they shout and scream at each other.

6. _____ : That's a neat idea.
   a. That's a great idea.
   b. That's a terrible idea.

Scene 3: "We were just wondering . . ."

UNDERSTUDIES

IN GROUPS OF THREE

SOUND OFF

4:03 - 5:15

A. With the sound off, watch the scene. Work with two other students to perform only the *actions* in the scene. Include these events:

MARILYN	ELLEN	PHILIP
• helps to make the bed	• helps to make the bed	• walks into the room and carries some hangers
• walks to the other side of the bed, near Ellen	• walks to the trunk	• walks to the trunk
• eats a banana		• puts a key in the lock of the trunk

SOUND ON

4:03 - 5:15

B. Now, with the sound on, watch the scene. Work with your group to say the following information. It is not important to repeat the characters' words exactly.

MARILYN	ELLEN	PHILIP
• asks Ellen about the trunk	• says she doesn't know what's inside the trunk	• says he wants to put some good hangers in Grandpa's closet
• greets Philip	• tells Philip about Susan's business trip	• says Grandpa will be disappointed about Susan
• asks Philip about the trunk	• tells Philip the trunk is locked	• says Susan reminds Grandpa of Grandma

C. Put together the actions and dialogue from Parts *A* and *B*. Practice the scene three times. Then perform it for the whole class.

UNDERSTUDIES

PREPARE

Create a "stage" at the front of the classroom. Label a desk or table as "the bed." In front of it, use a box or student desk to be "Grandpa's trunk." As props, use a rolled up sheet of paper as a "banana" and pens or pencils as "hangers." One of your keys can be "the key to Grandpa's trunk."

PARTICIPATE

1. Turn the sound off and play the scene (4:03 to 5:15).
2. With the class, read the instructions for part A and the lists of actions that Marilyn, Ellen, and Richard perform in the scene.
3. Have students work in groups of three. Ask different groups to use the props you have prepared and to demonstrate the actions of the scene in the correct sequence—without speaking.
4. Turn the sound on and play the scene again.
5. With the class, read the instructions for part B and the information for Marilyn, Ellen, and Richard.
6. Taking the characters one at a time, elicit appropriate dialogue for each item. Allow for variations. Encourage students to use their own ideas. It is not necessary for students to repeat the characters' words exactly.
7. Have the groups practice the dialogue.
8. With the class, read the instructions for part C. Have the groups practice the actions and dialogue together.
9. Have different groups perform the scene for the class.

EXTEND

The scene ends when Philip places the key in the keyhole. Recalling students' suggestions (during the Preview activity) about the trunk's contents, encourage students to extend the scene with new dialogue.

FOCUS IN: OPINIONS AND BELIEFS

PARTICIPATE

1. Play the "Focus In" segment (5:16 to 6:34).
2. Ask each of the following comprehension questions. The answers are given in parentheses.
   a. Who thinks Grandpa is independent? (Ellen)
   b. Who thinks Grandpa is funny? (Robbie)
   c. Who thinks Grandpa will miss being in Florida? (Robbie)
   d. Who thinks Grandpa will like being with the family? (Richard)
3. With the class, read the instructions for part A. Have students work in small groups to complete the activity. Encourage them to use the different expressions from the Conversation Box.
4. With the class, read the instructions for part B. Have each group think of three famous people and write the names on a piece of paper.
5. Write the expressions from both of the Conversation Boxes on the board.
6. Collect the papers and read the names to the class. Elicit opinions from the class about each person. Encourage students to agree or disagree.

ACT I INTERMISSION
PRONUNCIATION
INTONATION OF *EITHER/OR* QUESTIONS

PREPARE

1. Rewind the video to 1:54.
2. Write Ellen's question on the board: "Marilyn, you want coffee or tea?"

PARTICIPATE

1. With the class, read the explanation and play the line of dialogue beginning at 1:54.
2. With the class, practice the intonation of questions 1–6.
3. Have students work in pairs to practice saying the questions.
4. Copy the four incomplete questions from part B onto the board.
5. With the class, read the instructions for part B.
6. Read the following cues to the class. Have students choose one of the phrases on the board to begin an *either/or* question. Be sure to use the correct intonation in your cues. (Your voice rises on the first item. Your voice rises and falls on the second.) Possible student responses are given in parentheses.

   Teacher: married or single?
   Student: (Are you married or single?)
   Teacher: Coffee or tea?
   Student: (Do you want coffee or tea?)
   Teacher: stay home or go to the movies?
   Student: (Should we stay home or go to the movies?)
   Teacher: take a vacation next year or stay home?
   Student: (Will you take a vacation next year or stay home?)

7. Have students work with a partner to use the four incomplete questions to ask and answer other *either/or* questions. Encourage students to ask for information that they would really like to know.

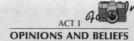

IN SMALL GROUPS

ACT I
OPINIONS AND BELIEFS

SOUND ON
5:16 - 6:34

A. Watch the "Focus in" segment two times. What kind of man is Grandpa? What do you imagine he's like? Tell your opinions and beliefs about Grandpa to the other members of your group. Begin your sentences with the expressions from the Conversation Box.

CONVERSATION BOX	
I think . . .	In my opinion . . .
I guess . . .	I believe . . .
I bet . . .	I suppose . . .

B. Now choose a famous person—someone everyone in your group knows. Tell your opinions and beliefs about this person. You may agree or disagree with the other students' ideas. Use the expressions from the Conversation Box below to agree or disagree with the opinions and beliefs of the other members of your group.

CONVERSATION BOX	
I agree.	I don't agree.
I think that's true.	I don't think that's true.

ACT I
INTERMISSION
PRONUNCIATION: Intonation of *either/or* Questions

IN PAIRS

SOUND ON
REWIND TO 1:54

Rewind the tape to 1:54 and listen to Ellen's question. She asks,

"Marilyn, you want coffee or tea?"

Note: The formal question is *Do you want coffee or tea?* In informal questions beginning with *Do you,* you sometimes don't use the auxiliary *do.*

When you ask someone to choose between two items, your voice goes up on the first item (*coffee*). Your voice goes up and then down on the second item (*tea*). The answer to Ellen's question is "Coffee, please" or "Tea, please."

A. With a partner, practice using the correct intonation to ask each of the following questions:

1. Do you want soup or salad?
2. Would like juice or a soft drink?
3. Will you wear a coat or a jacket?
4. Did you take a bus or a train?
5. Should we meet on Friday or Saturday?
6. Are you awake or asleep?

B. Ask your partner to make some real choices. Ask *either/or* questions. Begin your questions in each of the following ways:

1. Are you . . . ?
2. Should we . . . ?
3. Do you want . . . ?
4. Will you . . . ?

GRAMMAR AND EXPRESSIONS: Talking About Future Schedules

IN PAIRS

Near the beginning of Act I, Marilyn wants to know about Grandpa's schedule. She asks Ellen,

"When does he arrive?" We learn that *he arrives* at six o'clock this evening.

You often use the simple present tense (*arrive/arrives*) instead of the simple future tense (*will arrive*) to show that an event is on a schedule. Tell your partner some events on your schedule for the next few weeks. Use the simple present tense. Use some of the time expressions from the Conversation Box.

EXAMPLES
- I *have* an English test next Thursday.
- My birthday *is* the day after tomorrow.
- Tomorrow afternoon I *take* my sister to the airport.

CONVERSATION BOX	
tomorrow night	on (Tuesday night)
on (Saturday)	at (eight) o'clock
on (Sunday morning)	next (Wednesday)
on (Monday afternoon)	(two) weeks from (today)
the day after tomorrow	on (October ninth)

USEFUL LANGUAGE

In Act I, you heard ways to . . .

- express excitement:
  I am so excited!
  I'm very excited about his arrival.
- talk about a future event at a specific point in time:
  At this time tomorrow morning, Grandpa will be sitting in the kitchen with us.
- talk about future schedules:
  When does he arrive?

- express approval or agreement:
  That's for sure.
  That's a neat idea.
- express admiration:
  He's something!
- express an opinion or belief:
  I think . . .   I believe . . .
  I guess . . .   In my opinion . . .
  I bet . . .   I suppose . . .

- say two people are alike:
  She always reminds him of Grandma.
- ask indirectly about something:
  We were just wondering about this trunk. (= What's inside this trunk?)

↕

IN PAIRS

INSTANT ROLE-PLAYS

Practice this conversation with a partner:

The first day at a new job . . .

Employee: I'm so excited to work here!
Boss: We're happy you're here. Welcome to the company.
Employee: Thank you.
Boss: Will you miss your old friends?
Employee: Yes, but I'll make new ones.
Boss: Well, learning this job will take time. It's not easy.
Employee: That's for sure. When do I start?
Boss: Right now.

Then complete this conversation:

The first day at college . . .

A: Hi, I'm_____, your new roommate.
B:

A:
B:

A:
B:

A:
B:

GRAMMAR AND EXPRESSIONS

PARTICIPATE

1. With the class, read through the explanation, the examples, and the time expressions in the Conversation Box.
2. Have students work in pairs to tell their partner two truthful sentences for each time expression. As in the three examples, students should use the simple present tense to refer to future scheduled events.
3. Have students report to the class some events that *their partner* has scheduled. They will need to use the *-s* form to refer to their partner's future activities.

USEFUL LANGUAGE

PREPARE

With the students, read through the expressions in the box.

PARTICIPATE

1. Have students close their books.
2. Give each cue below. Elicit appropriate expressions from the class for each situation. The possible student answers are in parentheses.

Teacher: Let's have a class party next Friday.
Student: (That's a neat idea.)
Teacher: The President of the United States is coming to visit our class.
Student: (I'm so excited! *or* I'm very excited about his arrival.)
Teacher: What will you be doing at this time tomorrow?
Student: (I will be_____-ing . . . .)
Teacher: My friend is flying here by plane.
Student: (When does he/she arrive?)
Teacher: Grandpa is leaving Florida to live in New York. Why? Tell me your opinions.
Student: (I think . . . .   *or*   In my opinion . . . .   *or*   I bet . . . .   *or*   I suppose . . . .   *or*   I believe . . . .   *or*   I guess . . . .)

INSTANT ROLE-PLAYS

Repeat the role-play procedure outlined on page 7.

U.S. LIFE

PREPARE

Pre-teach: *to retire, retirement, retiree, active, to pursue, lifelong, hobby, in advance, income, pension, Social Security, federal government, sunbelt.*

PARTICIPATE

1. Have students read independently.
2. Ask for volunteers to read aloud.

YOUR TURN

Complete this exercise in small groups or with the entire class.

LESSON TWO

ACT II PREVIEW

PREPARE

1. Pre-teach: *to travel, indeed, to look forward to, permanently.*
2. Review the prepositions *on, with,* and *to.*

PARTICIPATE

1. With the class, read the instruction line and the words beneath each photo.
2. Play the Preview (6:39 to 7:21).
3. Have students complete the exercise.
4. Review answers.

FURTHER PRACTICE

Read these sentences to the class. Have students repeat the sentence including the missing preposition *on, with,* or *to.*

Teacher:

> I'm going * the zoo.
> My brother is going * me.
> It's not far * the zoo.
> We'll go * foot.

EXTEND: DOES HE WANT TO STAY?

Elicit student opinions.

READ AND DISCUSS

Read the paragraphs under "U.S. Life." Then discuss your answers to the questions under "Your Turn."

ON YOUR OWN

U.S. LIFE

Most Americans retire after the age of sixty. The usual age of retirement is 65, although some people retire at 55 or younger. Other Americans do not retire until they are in their seventies. This type of "late retirement" is more frequent now as population growth in the United States slows down, and the average age of the citizens increases.

Most senior citizens want to remain active after they retire. For many, retirement is an opportunity to pursue lifelong hobbies or interests.

Americans usually make plans for their retirement well in advance. Their income after retirement may include interest on bank savings and a company pension. Americans also receive Social Security payments from the federal government.

Many retirees move to warm parts of the country. The Sunbelt (the southern states) has many retirement communities. In some towns in Florida, for example, most of the citizens are retired persons.

IN SMALL GROUPS

YOUR TURN

1. At what age do workers usually retire in your country?
2. Do you have plans for retirement. If so, what are they?

Discover Florida living at
Glenmar Hills
FLORIDA'S BEAUTIFUL RETIREMENT COMMUNITY
...in Lauderhill, Florida
Come enjoy
GOLF•TENNIS•SWIMMING•BOATING•FISHING
BILLIARDS•ARTS AND CRAFTS
Custom-built homes from $45,000
For more information, call
1-800-555-3306

ACT II
PREVIEW
SOUND ON

6:39 - 7:21

Watch the preview to complete the sentences. Choose the correct preposition from the Word Box. Write the prepositions on the blank lines. The first answer is given.

1.

Grandpa travels __to__ New York City _____ the train and meets a woman named Elsa Tobin.

2.

They enjoy talking _____ each other.

WORD BOX

on

with

to

3.

Grandpa is looking forward _____ seeing his family. But does he want to stay _____ them permanently?

4.

"Are you going to live _____ them?"

ACT II
VIDEO GAMES

Scene 1: "Excuse me."

PAUSE
SOUND OFF

7:22 - 8:00

With the sound off, watch the scene and pause at the three times below. What are Elsa Tobin and Grandpa saying? Can you guess? Circle *a*, *b*, or *c*.

1.
PAUSE AT 7:39

2.
PAUSE AT 7:43

3.
PAUSE AT 7:51

Elsa Tobin:
a. Can I sit next to you?
b. Are you going far?
c. Is this seat taken?

Grandpa:
a. Oh, let me help you with this.
b. Allow me. I'm stronger than you are.
c. That's too heavy for you.

Grandpa:
a. Which seat do you want?
b. Do you want to sit by the window?
c. Ladies first.

Now, <u>with the sound on</u>, watch the scene again to check your answers.

Scene 2: "Small world."

LISTEN IN
SOUND ON

8:01 - 11:02

Read the statements below. Then watch the scene and listen to it carefully. Which of the following items are true according to the information in the scene? Put a check (✔) in the box <u>only if you are sure the sentence is true.</u>

☐ **1.** Elsa Tobin changed seats because a man was smoking.

☐ **2.** Elsa never lived outside Florida.

☐ **3.** Grandpa and Elsa are from the same town.

☐ **4.** Elsa's husband isn't traveling with her because he had to work.

☐ **5.** Grandpa sold his house to a young couple.

☐ **6.** Grandpa's wife died at the age of 61.

☐ **7.** Grandpa was married for 47 years.

☐ **8.** Elsa's husband is an engineer.

☐ **9.** Grandpa recently retired.

PAUSE

PREPARE
Pre-teach: *next to, taken* (a seat), *allow.*

PARTICIPATE
1. With the class, read the instruction line and the dialogue beneath each pause cue.
2. Turn the sound off and play scene 1 (7:22 to 8:00) without pausing.
3. Replay scene 1, pausing at the times indicated. Elicit answers from the class.
4. Turn the sound on and replay scene 1 to review answers.

LISTEN IN

PREPARE
Pre-teach: *aisle, to bother, small world, time off, to ship, destination, to be exact, anniversary, aerospace, construction, take your time.*

PARTICIPATE
1. With the class, read the instruction line and statements 1–9 below.
2. Play scene 2 (8:01 to 11:02).
3. Have students complete the exercise on their own.
4. Review student answers.
5. Replay the scene to check answers.
6. CULTURE NOTE: Mrs. Tobin said she moved because someone was smoking a cigarette and it bothered her. She is not unusual. Smoking in public places is becoming more and more restricted.

IN OTHER WORDS

PREPARE
Pre-teach: *coincidence.*

PARTICIPATE
1. With the class, read the instruction line and sentences 1–5 below, and review the expressions in the Word and Phrase Box.
2. Play scene 2 again.
3. Have students complete the exercise.
4. Review student answers.
5. Replay the scene to check answers.

SPLIT DIALOGUE

PREPARE
1. Divide the class into pairs of like abilities, A and B.
2. Pre-teach: *kids, can't wait* (to do something), *to mind* (not like) *something.*

PARTICIPATE
1. With the class, read the instruction line.
2. Play scene 3 (11:03 to 12:29).
3. Have students complete the exercise.
   Note: For pairs of more advanced levels, each student may be able to complete both Grandpa's and Elsa's dialogue in the time allotted.
4. Replay scene 3.
5. Review student answers.

EXTEND
Discussion: Pose this hypothetical situation to your students:
"Imagine you are retired and your family invites you to live with them. Would you accept? Why or why not?"

IN OTHER WORDS . . .

Read the following information from the scene. Which word or phrase does Grandpa or Mrs. Tobin use to express the <u>underlined</u> part of each sentence? Choose your answers from the Word and Phrase Box. Write each answer on the line below the underlined phrase.

1. Grandpa tells Mrs. Tobin that he's from Titusville, Florida. She says, "<u>What a coincidence!</u> I'm from Titusville, too."

2. Elsa tells Grandpa that her husband isn't traveling with her because he couldn't <u>stay away from work</u>.

3. Elsa says that she will soon celebrate her fortieth wedding anniversary. Grandpa says, "<u>That's great!</u>"

4. Grandpa sent his things to New York. "That's <u>where I'm going.</u>"

5. As Mrs. Tobin looks for her ticket, the conductor says, "<u>There's no need to hurry.</u>"

WORD AND PHRASE BOX

Take your time.
Congratulations!
take time off
my destination
Small world.

Scene 3: "I didn't want to be alone anymore!"

SPLIT DIALOGUE

IN PAIRS

SOUND ON

11:03 - 12:29

Watch the scene to complete the sentences below. Work with a partner. One of you will complete Grandpa's lines; the other will complete Elsa Tobin's. Choose the correct words from the Word Box. Two answers are given. Play the scene as many times as necessary.

GRANDPA
1. Do you have *family* in New York?
2. Yes, indeed. A _____ and his _____ and their three children—my _____.
3. I _____ _____ to see them!
4. _____.
5. Well . . . they want me to, but it's too early to know for sure. I'm pretty _____. I tried to teach my _____ the importance of _____, but I'm not sure I want to be _____. Some people don't mind being alone. I do.
6. I _____ because . . . I wanted to be with my family. I didn't want to be alone anymore!

WORD BOX

grandchildren
wife
son
family
friends
independence
alone
excited
independent
kids
retired
can't wait
understand
Yes
Permanently

ELSA TOBIN
1. No, no. But I do have very close *friends* in New York City. We like to go to the theater together. You said you have family in New York.
2. You must be _____.
3. Are you going to live with them?
4. _____?
5. I _____. But tell me. Why did you stop working?

Now watch the scene again. Check your answers with your partner. Then practice reading the dialogue together.

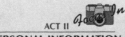

ACT II
PERSONAL INFORMATION

SOUND ON

12:30 - 14:30

Watch the "Focus In" segment two times. The second time, your teacher will pause after each line with a star, or asterisk (*). Take turns with your partner asking and answering each question with a star. Give personal answers.

What's your name?*
　Grandpa: My name is Stewart.
　　　　Malcolm Stewart.
Pleased to meet you.
What's your name?*
　Elsa: I'm Elsa Tobin. How do you do?
How do you do?
Where do you live?*
　Grandpa: Titusville.
Where do you live?*
　Elsa: Small World. I'm from
　　　　Titusville, too.
It's a small, small world.
How do you do?
Are you married? Yes or no?
Please tell me. Let me know.*

　Elsa: John and I celebrate our fortieth
　　　　anniversary next month.
Congratulations!
What do you do?
Are you a doctor, a farmer, a mailman?
A lawyer, an artist, a salesman?
A businessman or a preacher?
A high-school teacher?*
　Grandpa: I just retired.
Do you have family in New York?*
　Elsa: No.
Do you have family in New York?*
　Grandpa: Yes, indeed.
I'm pleased to meet you.
How do you do?
I'm pleased to meet you.

FOCUS IN: PERSONAL INFORMATION

PREPARE
Divide the class into pairs, A and B.

PARTICIPATE
1. With the class, read the instruction line and the words to the song.
2. Play the "Focus In" segment (12:30 to 14:30), pausing at the questions(*) indicated.
3. Replay the segment, encouraging students to sing along, while incorporating their own responses.

ACT II INTERMISSION
GRAMMAR AND EXPRESSIONS

PREPARE

1. This exercise practices *too, either,* and *but* to express similarities and differences. To succeed in this exercise, students need a firm grasp of the auxiliaries used for different tenses. It is a good idea to review auxiliaries through the use of short answers. Ask questions such as these to elicit short answers:

Do you study English?

Are you single?

Will you be home tomorrow?

Is your brother married?

Do your friends speak English?

Will you visit them this weekend?

Do you drive a car?

Are your grandparents living?

Do they live with you?

Does your mother work?

Continue to ask yes or no questions with the verb *to be* and other verbs until students have a firm grasp of the auxiliaries used. Use whatever verb tenses your students have mastered.

2. Divide the class into pairs, A and B.

PARTICIPATE

1. With the class, read the examples and instruction line A.

2. Replay Act II, 7:22 to 12:29. Have students listen carefully for ways in which Elsa and Grandpa are alike, and ways in which they are different.

3. Have each pair write three examples for part A.

4. With the class, read instruction line B.

5. Have students complete the exercise.

6. With the class, read instruction line C.

7. Group together two pairs of similar ability. Have students complete exercise C.

EXTEND

With students still in groups of four, have them find other similarities and differences among the members of their group.

_____ ACT II _____

IN PAIRS

INTERMISSION

GRAMMAR AND EXPRESSIONS: Similarities and Differences

In Act II, Elsa and Grandpa discover that they may have something in common—something that is the same about them. Here is their dialogue:

Elsa: I'm from Florida.
Grandpa: I am, too. (= I am from Florida, too.)

• To express similarities—something that is the same about people or things, use *and* and *too.* It is not necessary to repeat the words after an auxiliary or the verb *be*:

Elsa is from Florida. Grandpa is from Florida. → Elsa is from Florida, *and* Grandpa is, *too.*

Elsa will go to New York. Grandpa will go to New York.→ Elsa will go to New York, *and* Grandpa will, *too.*

• To express similarities when the verb is negative, use *either* instead of *too*:

Grandpa doesn't like staying at home. Elsa doesn't like staying at home. → Grandpa doesn't like staying at home, *and* Elsa doesn't, *either.*

• To expresses differences, use *but*:

Grandpa has family in New York. Elsa doesn't have family in New York. → Grandpa has family in New York, *but* Elsa doesn't.

Grandpa won't go back to Florida. Elsa will go back to Florida. → Grandpa won't go back to Florida, *but* Elsa will.

A. With your partner, compare Elsa and Grandpa. How are they similar? How are they different? Say your answers by completing the following three sentences in many ways. Don't repeat unnecessary words.

1. Elsa _____, and Grandpa _____, too.
2. Elsa _____, and Grandpa _____, either.
3. Elsa _____, but Grandpa _____.

B. Now find out some similarities and differences between your partner and yourself. List these below.

SIMILARITIES	DIFFERENCES
We both _____.	I _____. My partner _____.
We both _____.	I _____. My partner _____.
We both _____.	I _____. My partner _____.

IN TWO PAIRS

C. Now get together with another pair of students. Tell them about the similarities and differences between you and your partner (from Part B, above). Complete the following sentences. Then the other pair of students will complete the sentences, too. Don't repeat unnecessary words.

1. I _____, and (your partner's name) _____.too.
2. I _____, and (your partner's name) _____, either.
3. I _____, but (your partner's name) _____.

USEFUL LANGUAGE

In Act I, you heard ways to . . .

- offer help:
  Let me help you with this.
- ask for help:
  Would you kindly hold these keys?

- tell someone not to hurry:
  Take your time.
- express similarities:
  I am, too.
- respond to good news:
  Congratulations!

- express excitement about a future event:
  I can't wait to see them!
- say something doesn't bother someone:
  Some people don't mind being alone.

IN GROUPS OF THREE

INSTANT ROLE-PLAYS

Practice this conversation with two other students:

At a concert hall . . .

A: I can't wait for the concert to begin! I'm really excited.

B: I am, too. I don't mind sitting way up here. We can see very well.

C: Excuse me. I think you're sitting in our seats.

Then complete this conversation:

On an airplane . . .

A: I can't wait _____! I _____

B: I _____, too. I don't mind _____.

C: Excuse me. _____

ACT III
PREVIEW

SOUND ON

14:35 - 15:10

Watch the preview to complete the sentences. Choose the correct words from the Word Box. Write the words on the blank lines.

1.

In the third Act, Grandpa _____ in _____.

WORD BOX

Presents

opens

arrives

full

trunk

me

surprises

New York

3.

" _____ —for _____ ?"

2.

And the night is _____ of _____.

4.

And Grandpa _____ the _____.

What's inside the trunk?

USEFUL LANGUAGE

PREPARE

Read through and explain the expressions to your students.

PARTICIPATE

1. Have students close their books.
2. Make the statements below. Elicit responses from the class. The possible student answers are in parentheses.

Teacher: Guess what? I was named "Teacher of the Year!"

Student: (Congratulations!)

Teacher: I'll bring pictures of the award ceremony to show the class.

Student: (I can't wait to see them.)

Teacher: (Try to lift the desk.) Boy this desk is heavy!

Student: (Let me help you with this.)

Teacher: (Act nervous and hurried.) I can't find today's video tape.

Student: (Take your time.)

Teacher: Guess what? The subway's broken down. We have to walk home. Do you mind?

Student: (I don't mind walking.)

INSTANT ROLE-PLAYS

PREPARE

Divide the class into groups of three, A, B, and C.

PARTICIPATE

Repeat the role-play procedure outlined on page 7.

LESSON THREE
ACT III PREVIEW

PREPARE

1. Pre-teach: *here we are, presents.*
2. With the class, read the instruction line and the words beneath each photo.

PARTICIPATE

1. With the class, read the instruction line.
2. Play the Preview (14:35 to 15:10).
3. Have students complete the exercise.
4. Review correct answers.

ARRIVING IN NEW YORK CITY

PREPARE

Pre-teach: *Amtrak* (the American passenger train service), *announce, belongings, Big Apple* (the nickname of New York City).

PARTICIPATE

1. With the class, read the instruction line.
2. Have students listen to the announcement (15:11 to 15:24). Have students follow the announcement as it plays.
3. Repeat instruction 2.
4. Have students complete the exercise on their own.
5. Review student answers.
6. Play the announcement again and read along with the announcer.

PAUSE

PREPARE

Pre-teach: *finally, trip, to look somebody up* (to contact somebody in the future), *caring, say hello to* (someone) *for me.*

PARTICIPATE

1. With the class, read the instruction line and the dialogue beneath each pause cue.
2. Turn the sound off and play the scene segment (15:25 to 15:54).
3. Replay scene 1, pausing at the times indicated. Elicit answers from the class.
4. Turn the sound on and replay the scene segment to review answers.

ACT III

VIDEO GAMES

Scene 1: "And have a good stay in the Big Apple."

ARRIVING IN NEW YORK CITY

SOUND ON
PICTURE OFF

15:11 - 15:24

With the sound on and the picture off, play the video. Can you understand the announcer's voice? What is he saying? Complete the sentences below. You may listen as many times as necessary. Then play the scene with both the picture and the sound on to check your answers.

"Ladies and gentlemen, Amtrak _____ happy _____ announce _____ arrival _____ New York City. _____ train _____ _____ stopping _____ five minutes. Please check _____ be sure _____ _____ _____ belongings. _____ _____ _____ good stay _____ _____ Big Apple. Thanks."

PAUSE

SOUND OFF

15:25 - 15:54

With the sound off, watch the scene and pause at the three times below. What are Elsa Tobin and Grandpa saying? Can you guess? Circle a, b, or c.

1.

PAUSE AT 15:25

2.

PAUSE AT 15:32

3.

PAUSE AT 15:47

Elsa Tobin: a. Well, here we are.
b. When will we get there?
c. Finally! It was a very long trip.

Grandpa: a. Would you like to join us for dinner?
b. Please look us up. We're in the phone book.
c. I'd like to go to the theater with you and your friends.

Elsa Tobin: a. You're very lucky to have a caring family.
b. Take care of your family.
c. Say hello to your family for me.

Now, with the sound on, watch the scene again to check your answers.

Scene 2: "This one really brings back memories."

IN PAIRS

WHO AND WHEN?

SOUND ON

15:55 — 18:10

A. Read the lines below. Who says each line? Write *Grandpa, Richard, Robbie, Ellen, Marilyn,* or *Philip* in each blank space. The first answer is given.

a.	*Ellen*	: That's a great idea, Grandpa! Philip needs a day off.
b.		: Oh, I'm sorry Susan isn't here.
c.		: When can we go fishing?
d.		: Pleasant dreams.
e.		: Let's give him our presents—now.
f.		: You name the day.
g.		: She called to say the plane was delayed.
h.		: Ellen and I'll take you to your room.
i.		: I'd better unpack.
j.		: From me and Marilyn.
k.		: Presents—for me?
l.		: I'm sure glad you're here, Grandpa.
m.		: We'll go fishing soon, and we'll take your dad with us.
n.		: This one really brings back memories.

B. Now work together to put the lines in Part A in the correct order. Number the lines from 1 to 14. Write each number in the correct box.

WITH THE WHOLE CLASS

THANKS FOR THE MEMORIES

Bring to class a photo that "really brings back memories" for you. Tell the class about your photo. Why does it bring back memories?

WHO AND WHEN?

PREPARE
Pre-teach: *day off, to unpack, pleasant dreams.*

PARTICIPATE
1. Divide the class into pairs, A and B.
2. With the class, read instruction line A and the lines of dialogue a–n.
3. Play scene 2 (15:55 to 18:10).
4. Have students complete the exercise.
5. Replay scene 2, if necessary.
6. Review answers.
7. With the class, read instruction line B.
8. Replay scene 2.
9. Have students complete the exercise.
10. Review answers.

THANKS FOR THE MEMORIES
1. Ask students to show the class the photos of themselves and a family member they have brought to class.
2. Ask these questions:
   Who are the people in the picture?
   Where was the picture taken?
   Who took it?
   How long ago was it taken?
   What else happened that day?
3. Have the class ask the questions.
   Cue questions with the first words: Who...?
   Where...? How long ago...? What else...?

UNDERSTUDIES

PREPARE

1. Pre-teach: *it doesn't work* (does not operate), *to research, family tree, fabulous*.
2. Recreate the "stage" at the front of the classroom used in the UNDERSTUDIES exercise on p. 35.

PARTICIPATE

1. Divide the class into groups of four, A, B, C and D.
2. Play scene 3 (18:11 to 19:55).
3. With the class, read the instruction line and the actions that Grandpa, Ellen, Philip and Susan perform in the scene.
4. Ask students to choose a character and replay scene 3.
5. Taking the characters one at a time, elicit the dialogue. Allow for variations. Encourage students to use their own ideas. Avoid repeating the actual dialogue word for word. Replay scene 3, if necessary.
6. Have the groups practice the dialogue.
7. Ask for a volunteer group to perform actions and dialogue for the class. Ask for other groups to volunteer. Allow as many groups as wish to volunteer to do so.

IN FACT

PREPARE

Review the use of the simple past tense auxiliary *did/didn't* in short answers.

PARTICIPATE

1. Divide the class into pairs, A and B.
2. Replay scene 3.
3. Have students complete the exercise.
4. Review student answers.

Scene 3: "A gift from me."

IN GROUPS OF FOUR

UNDERSTUDIES

SOUND ON

18:11 - 19:55

Watch the scene and listen to it carefully. Work in groups of four to act out the scene. It is not important to repeat the characters' words exactly. Include this information:

GRANDPA	ELLEN	PHILIP	SUSAN
• asks Philip for the key, tries it, and says he sent the wrong one	• says the family tree is an exciting gift	• says he has the key, but it doesn't unlock the trunk	• rushes into the room and gives Grandpa a hug
• finds the right key in his pocket, opens the trunk, and says he researched the family tree	• thanks Grandpa and gives him a hug	• accepts the gift and says it's fabulous	• tells Grandpa she's happy to see him
• greets Susan and says she looks like Grandma	• tells Grandpa she knows he will be happy living with them	• says he didn't know Grandpa's grandfather was from Germany	
• says he doesn't feel alone anymore		• tells Grandpa he'll be happy with the family	

After you practice the scene, you may perform it for the whole class.

IN PAIRS

IN FACT

With the sound on, watch the scene again. Then complete this activity with a partner. Take turns asking and answering the questions. If your answer is *no*, give the correct answer. The first two answers are given.

1. Does Philip have the right key?
   No, he doesn't. He has the wrong key.
2. Did Grandpa send the wrong key?
   Yes, he did.
3. Do Ellen and Philip like the gift?
4. Did the family tree take Grandpa a month to prepare?
5. Did Grandpa's father come from France?
6. Did Susan get to the house too late to see Grandpa?
7. Does Susan look like Grandma?
8. Will Grandpa like living with his family?

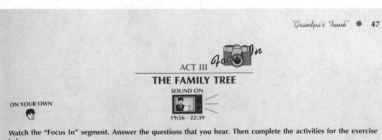

ACT III

THE FAMILY TREE

SOUND ON
19:56 · 22:39

ON YOUR OWN

Watch the "Focus In" segment. Answer the questions that you hear. Then complete the activities for the exercise below.

Malcolm   Bernice

Philip   Ellen

Marilyn   Richard   Susan   Robbie

The Stewarts

YOUR FAMILY TREE

A. Make your own family tree. Write the name of your relative on the line below each family member.

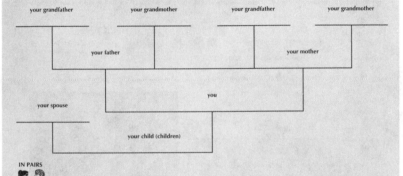

your grandfather   your grandmother   your grandfather   your grandmother

your father   your mother

your spouse   you

your child (children)

IN PAIRS

B. Work with a partner. Tell each other something about the members of your family. Then answer each of these questions about your grandparents.

1. Where did they come from?
2. What kind of work did they do?
3. When did they get married?
4. What were their favorite activities?
5. How many children did they have?
6. What do you remember most about them?

FOCUS IN: THE FAMILY TREE

PREPARE

Pre-teach: *peace and quiet, lonely, nearby, talented, intelligent, loveable.*

PARTICIPATE

1. With the class, read the instruction line.
2. Play the "Focus In" segment (19:56 to 22:39).
3. Replay the segment, pausing at the questions, and elicit student answers. (Questions occur at 22:04, 22:14, and 22:23.)

YOUR FAMILY TREE

PARTICIPATE

1. With the class, read instruction line A.
2. Have students complete the exercise.
3. Divide the class into pairs, A and B.
4. Read instruction line B and questions 1–6.
5. Have student B ask student A questions 1–6, and student A ask student B the questions in turn.

ACT III FINALE
USEFUL LANGUAGE

PREPARE
Read through and explain the expressions to your students.

PARTICIPATE
1. Have students close their books.
2. Make the statements below. Elicit responses from the class. The possible student answers are in parentheses.

Teacher: I miss my friend.
Student: (I'm sorry your friend isn't here.)
Teacher: I'm going to bed now.
Student: (Pleasant dreams.)
Teacher: Tell me I look like a friend of yours.
Student: (You look just like my friend.)
Teacher: (Hold up a photo.) Here's a picture of you from five years ago.
Student: (This picture really brings back memories.)
Teacher: I just arrived here after ten years away.
Student: (I'm so happy to see you! *or* I'm sure glad you're here!)
Teacher: I'm visiting Los Angeles for two days.
Student: (Have a good stay.)
Teacher: Want to have lunch together?
Student: (You name the day.)
Teacher: I'd like to see you again sometime.
Student: (Please look me up.)

TELEPLAYS

PREPARE
Review the use of the simple future tense.

PARTICIPATE
1. Divide the class into small groups.
2. With the class, read instruction line A.
3. To help students get started, write these subjects on the board: *travel, computers, television, music, pollution, space exploration*.
4. Have students say things about each.
5. With the class, read instruction line B. Allow students to work individually or in pairs.
6. Ask for volunteers to read their work to the class.

U.S. LIFE

PREPARE
Pre-teach: *senior citizens, similar, choice, lifelong, mate, service organization*.

PARTICIPATE
1. Have students read independently.
2. Ask these comprehension questions:
   a. What two situations may force senior citizens to live with their families?
   b. Name some things retired citizens do.

YOUR TURN
Complete this exercise in small groups or with the entire class.

STORYWRITER
1. With the class, read the instruction line.
2. Have students choose which of the subjects they wish to write about.

ACT III
FINALE

USEFUL LANGUAGE

In Act III, you heard ways to . . .

• wish someone a happy visit:
Have a good stay.
• invite someone to visit you:
Please look us up.
• accept an invitation:
You name the day.

• talk about a memory after seeing something or someone:
This [picture] really brings back memories.
• express regret:
I'm sorry Susan isn't here.
• say you are pleased to see someone:
I'm sure glad you're here.
I'm so happy to see you!

• wish someone a good night's sleep:
Pleasant dreams.
• express a similarity:
You look just like Grandma.

IN SMALL GROUPS

TELEPLAYS

A. With your group, imagine that you are all sitting with your grandparents—and the time is fifty years ago. Tell your "young" grandparents about "the future." How will life be different?
B. Be TV writers. Write a script for your conversation in Part A.

READ AND DISCUSS
Read the paragraphs under "U.S. Life." Then discuss your answers to the questions under "Your Turn."

ON YOUR OWN

U.S. LIFE
In the U.S., senior citizens often have to make decisions similar to those that Grandpa must make. For example, will they live permanently with their family? Or are they too independent? Will they prefer to live alone? Many older Americans must face these choices after the death of a lifelong mate, or if they have health problems of their own.

Senior citizens in the U.S. usually like to be active. Retired workers sometimes join service organizations. For example, retired businesspeople may become members of a group that gives advice to new businesses. Other retired persons may volunteer to work at libraries, schools, museums, or hospitals.

ON YOUR OWN

✎ STORYWRITER
By yourself, write about one of the following:
• Write the story of this episode for someone who didn't see it.
• Describe Grandpa. How is he like an older member of your family? How is he different?

IN SMALL GROUPS

YOUR TURN
1. Do you have an older family member living with you? If you do, tell your group about this relative.
2. Would you like to live with your children after you retire? Why, or why not?
3. Who is your favorite older relative?

STORYWRITER (*continued*)
3. Give students ten minutes to write.
4. Collect and exchange papers. Have students stand up and read the papers of their classmates.

● ● ● ● ● ● ● ● ● ●
E P I S O D E   4

"A Piece of Cake"

In this unit, you will practice . . .

ways of saying something is easy or difficult
pronouncing *can* or *can't* before verbs
using *How much* and *How many*

ACT I
PREVIEW

SOUND ON

24:50 - 25:25

Watch the preview to complete the sentences. Choose the correct words from the Word Box. Write the words on the blank lines. The first answer is given.

1.

"My new *exercise* class is so _____."

2.

"I think _____ is _____."

3.

So they _____ a _____

4.

"I bet I can _____ one _____ in your _____ this morning and not _____ a thing."

WORD BOX
make
go
bet
hour
hard
aerobics
class
feel
exercise
easy

Who's going to win the bet?

"A Piece of Cake" ● 49

EPISODE 4: "A Piece of Cake"

SUMMARY
Marilyn challenges Richard to try her aerobics class.

LANGUAGE
• ways of saying something is easy or difficult
• pronouncing *can* or *can't* before verbs
• using *how much* and *how many*

U.S. LIFE
• exercise and health

ADVANCE PLANNING
• Ask students to think about a situation in their lives when someone played a joke on them.

LESSON ONE

ACT I PREVIEW

PREPARE
Pre-teach: *aerobics, exercise* (physical), *make a bet, go* (perform), *not feel a thing* (not suffer pain).

PARTICIPATE
1. With the class, read the instruction line, the words beneath the photos, and the words in the Word Box.
2. Have students watch the entire Preview without writing.
3. Play the Preview (24:50 to 25:25).
4. Have students complete the exercise.
5. Play the Preview again so students can review their answers.

EXTEND: WHO'S GOING TO WIN THE BET?
1. Teach the adjectives *strength* and *endurance*.
2. Ask students which quality they admire the most.
3. Which character, Richard or Marilyn, exemplifies strength and which endurance?

BODY LANGUAGE

PREPARE

1. Pre-teach: *kidding, serious, worried, sure, convinced, not convinced.* Write the words on the board.
2. Introduce the idea of *body language* by expressing the words above through facial expressions and actions your students will recognize.

PARTICIPATE

1. With the class, read the instruction line.
2. Turn the sound off and play scene 1 without pausing (25:26 to 27:48).
3. Replay scene 1 and pause at the times indicated. Elicit answers from the class. Encourage discussion.

FURTHER PRACTICE

Pre-teach and then write on the board these adjectives:

alert, sleepy

interested, bored

enthusiastic, apathetic

hungry, full

confused, clear

contented, restless

UNDERSTUDIES

PREPARE

Pre-teach: *exhausted, beginners, intermediate and advanced* (classes), *nonstop, no problem, without a doubt, it's a snap.*

PARTICIPATE

1. Divide the class into pairs, A and B.
2. With the class, read the instruction line and the actions that Marilyn and Richard perform in the scene.
3. Ask students to choose a character.
4. Turn the sound on and play scene 1 again.
5. Taking the characters one at a time, elicit the dialogue. Allow for variations. Encourage students to use their own ideas. Avoid repeating the actual dialogue word for word. Replay scene 1, if necessary.
6. Have the groups practice the dialogue.
7. Ask for a volunteer group to perform actions and dialogue for the class. Ask for other groups to volunteer. Allow as many groups as wish to volunteer to do so.

ACT I
VIDEO GAMES

Scene 1: "It's a snap."

BODY LANGUAGE

SOUND OFF

25:26 - 27:48

Body language means the way people stand, sit, or move. Body language often shows a person's real feelings. With the sound off, watch the scene. Look at Marilyn's and Richard's body language and pause at the times below. Circle *a* or *b* to show the way Marilyn and Richard feel.

1.
PAUSE AT 26:08
Marilyn feels _____.
a. sad   b. tired

2.
PAUSE AT 26:20
Richard feels _____.
a. sad   b. happy

3.
PAUSE AT 26:58
Richard is _____.
a. kidding   b. serious

4.
PAUSE AT 27:10
Marilyn _____.
a. agrees   b. disagrees

5.
PAUSE AT 27:39
Richard is _____.
a. worried   b. sure

6.
PAUSE AT 27:45
Marilyn is _____.
a. convinced   b. not convinced

Now, **with the sound on**, play the scene again and check your answers.

UNDERSTUDIES

IN PAIRS

SOUND ON

25:26 - 27:48

Watch the scene again and listen to it carefully. Work with a partner to act out the scene. It is not important to repeat Marilyn's and Richard's words exactly. Include these events:

MARILYN	RICHARD
• arrives home after her aerobics class	• says he could easily work out in Marilyn's aerobics class
• talks to Richard about her class	
• tells Richard the day and time of the next aerobics class	• agrees to go to the aerobics class tomorrow morning at ten o'clock

After you practice the scene, you may perform it for the whole class.

Scene 2: "It's going to be a piece of cake."

WITH THE WHOLE CLASS

THE SUBTEXT

SOUND ON
27:49 - 29:05

1 I don't think you're so strong.

2 Would you like to find out who's right?

3 That's a good idea.

Read Marilyn's and Richard's thoughts above. Then watch the scene and listen to their conversation. What do Marilyn and Richard say to express these thoughts? Tell your teacher to stop the tape when you hear each answer.

THE BET

What's the bet? Write *Marilyn* or *Richard* on the blank lines.

1. If _____ can exercise for one hour with no problem, then _____ will cook dinner for the entire family.
2. If _____ can't exercise for one hour, then _____ will cook dinner for the entire family.

Scene 3: "It's all set."

LISTEN IN

SOUND ON
29:06 - 30:05

Read the statements below. Then watch the scene and listen to it carefully. Which of the following items are true according to the information in the scene? Put a check (✓) in the box <u>only if you are sure the sentence is true.</u>

☐ **1.** Jack Davis is the boss at the aerobics center.

☐ **2.** There are three aerobics classes each day.

☐ **3.** Before joining a class, students must write some information.

☐ **4.** Richard will photograph the class.

☐ **5.** Marilyn will watch Richard exercise.

☐ **6.** Susan will come for dinner.

☐ **7.** Richard will bicycle to the class.

THE SUBTEXT

PREPARE
Pre-teach: *no sweat, are you kidding?, a piece of cake, entire, instructor.*

PARTICIPATE
1. With the class, read the thought bubbles around the photo and the instruction line.
2. Play scene 2 (27:49 to 29:05). Students may ask you to pause in several different places for the same answer. Ask the student what Marilyn or Richard said. Then go on. Answers may vary. Encourage students to explain their answers.

THE BET

PARTICIPATE
1. Cue the video to 28:33.
2. With the class, read the instruction line and sentences 1 and 2.
3. Play the segment 28:33 to 28:47.
4. Have students complete the exercise.
5. Replay the segment, if necessary.
6. Review student answers.

LISTEN IN

PREPARE
Pre-teach: *forms, on my way over, all set* (arranged).

PARTICIPATE
1. With the class, read the instruction line and statements 1–7 below.
2. Play scene 3 (29:06 to 30:05).
3. Have students complete the exercise on their own.
4. Review student answers.
5. Replay the scene to check answers.

FOCUS IN: IDIOMS IN ACTION

PREPARE
Pre-teach: *rough, difficult, tough, hard.*

PARTICIPATE

1. With the class, read instruction line A.
2. Play the "Focus In" segment (30:06 to 32:06).
3. Replay the segment, encouraging students to sing along. (Replay as many times as you like.)
4. Notice that a male voice alternates with a female voice in the song. Divide your class into two groups and assign a part to each.
5. Replay the segment and sing along.
6. With the class, read instruction line B.
7. Pair up students from each of the two groups above. Have each fill in the box corresponding to their part in the song.
8. With the class, read instruction line C, the examples, and pre-teach the expressions in the Conversation Box.
9. Using the cartoon at the bottom of p. 52, elicit more examples from students of the form: "Can you . . . ?"
10. Have students complete the exercise.

EXTEND

1. Write these role-play pairs on the board:
   a. soccer instructor—new soccer tryout
   b. army recruitment officer—new recruit
   c. ballet dance instructor—new dance student
2. Taking the pairs one at a time, elicit verbs of physical activity or movement that each situation (soccer, army training, or dance) requires. Write these on the board under the appropriate pair.
3. Divide the class into pairs, A and B.
4. Have each pair choose a, b, or c above and create dialogue for an interview scene. The soccer instructor, army recruitment officer, and dance instructor will ask questions to the candidate to see if he or she is able to do the activity.
5. Ask for volunteers to perform their interview for the class.

ACT I

IDIOMS IN ACTION

WITH THE WHOLE CLASS

SOUND ON

30:06 - 32:06

A. Watch the "Focus In" segment. Then watch it again and sing along.

IN PAIRS

B. With a partner, try to remember the different ways to say *It's easy* and *It's difficult.* List each of those expressions in the correct box below. One answer is given.

It's easy.
It's a piece of cake.

It's difficult.

C. Ask your partner some questions about his or her physical abilities. Begin each question with *Can you . . . ?* If your partner's answer is *yes,* he or she will answer with one of the expressions from the first box above. If the answer is *no,* your partner can use one of the expressions from the second box above or from the Conversation Box below. Here are two examples:

A: *Can you* hold your breath for a minute?
B: Yes, it's a piece of cake.

A: *Can you* swim for an hour without stopping?
B: *No way!*

CONVERSATION BOX
No way!
You've got to be kidding!
Not on your life!
Not in a million years!

ACT I
INTERMISSION

USEFUL LANGUAGE

In Act I, you heard ways to . . .

- express a possibility:
  I could work out in your class . . .
- say something is easy:
  No problem.
  It's a snap.
  No sweat.
  It's a piece of cake.

- say something is difficult:
  It's rough.
  It's tough.
- express certainty:
  . . . without a doubt
  I bet I can . . .
- say to telephone someone:
  Give him a call.

- say you're leaving for a place:
  I'm on my way over.
- remind someone about something:
  And that includes Susan.
  Don't you forget.
- say something is arranged:
  It's all set.

↕

IN PAIRS

INSTANT ROLE-PLAYS

Practice this conversation with a partner:

At home . . .

A. I'm on my way to the store. Is there anything you'd like me to get?

B. Yes. Could you stop at the bakery and pick up a chocolate cake?

A. A chocolate cake?

B. Yes. It's Marion's birthday. We're having a party.

A. Oh, I bet she'll be surprised. Did you invite everyone?

B. It's all set.

Then complete this conversation:

In class . . .

Student: I bet I can finish this entire test in twenty minutes.

Teacher:

Student:

Teacher:

Student:

Teacher:

READ AND DISCUSS

Read the paragraphs under "U.S. Life." Then discuss your answers to the questions under "Your Turn."

ON YOUR OWN

U.S. LIFE

These days, Americans are paying attention to their health. They are eating right and exercising to stay **in shape. Aerobics** is a popular form of exercise in the United States. This type of exercise helps breathing and builds a strong heart. Jogging, swimming, and bicycle riding are just three kinds of aerobic exercise.

Americans are also watching their diet. Many people in the U.S. are eating food with less fat, salt, and sugar. Products without **cholesterol,** such as oat bran, are becoming very popular with Americans.

IN SMALL GROUPS

YOUR TURN

1. Do you exercise to stay in shape? What types of exercises do you do? Demonstrate them for your group.
2. Do you ever make bets? If so, what was the last bet you made?

ACT I INTERMISSION
USEFUL LANGUAGE

PREPARE
Read through and explain the expressions to your students.

PARTICIPATE
1. Have students close their books.
2. Make the statements below. Elicit responses from the class. The possible student answers are in parentheses.

Teacher:	My brother-in-law is in town. I just got his telephone number.
Student:	(Give him a call.)
Teacher:	Is this lesson difficult?
Student:	(It's a snap, It's a piece of cake, etc. *or* It's rough, It's difficult, etc.)
Teacher:	(Mime talking on the telephone.) Why don't you come over to my house now?
Student:	(Ok. I'm on my way over.)
Teacher:	Are you sure you can run a mile?
Student:	(Without a doubt. *or* I bet I can.)
Teacher:	I promised I would bring you all a surprise tomorrow, and I will.
Student:	(Don't you forget.)
Teacher:	Remember our class party? Did you make all the plans?
Student:	(It's all set.)

INSTANT ROLE-PLAYS

Repeat the role-play procedure outlined on page 7.

U.S. LIFE

PREPARE
Pre-teach: *to pay attention to, to stay in shape, to watch one's diet, products, cholesterol, oat bran.*

PARTICIPATE
1. Have students read independently.
2. Ask for volunteers to read aloud.
3. Ask these comprehension questions:
   a. Name three types of aerobic exercise.
   b. What foods are harmful if we eat too much of them?

YOUR TURN
Complete this exercise in small groups or with the entire class.

LESSON TWO

ACT II PREVIEW

PREPARE

Pre-teach: *free, excellent, ideal, condition, to earn, in exchange.*

PARTICIPATE

1. With the class, read the instruction line and summaries A, B, and C.
2. Turn the sound off and play the Preview (32:12 to 32:59).
3. Have students choose A, B, or C. Discuss the reasons for their choice.
4. Turn the sound on and replay the Preview to review answers.

EXTEND: WHO'S GOING TO WIN THE BET?

Hint: Richard tricked Marilyn. Will he tell her the truth later?

HEALTH FORM

PREPARE

1. Pre-teach: *blood pressure, physical* (examination), *interesting, nope, What do you do for a living?, the American scene* (modern life in America), *advertising, anytime.*
2. CULTURE NOTE: A fitness center is a place where people go for exercise classes. Some centers insist that new applicants have a brief physical examination to make sure they are physically able to perform in the class. This also helps protect the center against legal liability in the case of an accident.

PARTICIPATE

1. With the class, read the instruction line and go over the health form.
2. With books closed, play scene 1 (33:00 to 34:36) without pausing.
3. Have students complete the exercise as they listen to scene 1 again.
4. Replay scene 1 to review answers.

ACT II
PREVIEW

SOUND OFF

32:12 - 32:59

Read the three summaries below. Then, with the sound off, watch the preview. Guess which summary is correct. Circle *A, B,* or *C.*

A	B	C
Jack Davis says Richard is in very good condition and doesn't need to do aerobics. Instead, Jack offers Richard $200 to photograph the class. When Richard gets home, he tells Marilyn that he earned $200. He lost the bet because he didn't exercise. But he is happy because he has enough money to take the family to dinner at a nice restaurant.	Jack Davis wants some photos of his class. He offers Richard free lessons in exchange for photographing the class. Richard agrees. When Richard gets home, he tells Marilyn that they are going to get a month of free dancing lessons.	Jack Davis wants some photos of his class. He offers Richard free lessons in exchange for photographing an aerobics class. Richard agrees. When Richard gets home, he doesn't tell Marilyn what happened. She thinks he exercised. Marilyn is surprised to see that Richard isn't tired.

Now, with the sound on, watch the preview to check your answer.

ACT II
VIDEO GAMES

Scene 1: "Maybe you can photograph a class..."

HEALTH FORM

SOUND ON

33:00 - 34:36

Watch the scene and listen to it carefully. Use the information from the scene to fill in this health form for Richard.

Name: _____
Occupation: _____
Age: **30** Sex: M ☐ F ☐
Blood Pressure: (Sitting) _____ over _____
Blood Pressure: (Standing) _____ over _____
Date of last complete physical: _____
Do you have any back problems? Yes ☐ No ☐
Do you have any knee problems? Yes ☐ No ☐

IN TWO GROUPS

Scene 2: *"Stretch up."*

MOVE TO THE MUSIC

SOUND ON
34:37 - 36:05

Watch the scene and listen to it carefully. Then follow the instructions for your group.

GROUP A

Look at the drawings of the exercises done in Jack Davis' aerobics class. Find the correct word or phrase below to describe each exercise. Write the letter of the correct answer in the circle at the top left of each drawing.

a. push
b. tango
c. stretch left
d. stretch right
e. sunrise
f. twist

GROUP B

Look at the drawings of the exercises done in Jack Davis' aerobics class. What is the correct order of the exercises? Write *1, 2, 3, 4, 5,* or *6* in the box at the top right of each drawing.

WITH THE WHOLE CLASS

Watch the scene again. Then stand up and exercise along with the video! Name each exercise as you do it.

MOVE TO THE MUSIC

PREPARE

Note: This exercise teaches words that describe different physical exercises. Instead of pre-teaching the vocabulary, allow students to learn the meaning of the words from context.

PARTICIPATE

1. Play scene 2 (34:37 to 36:05).
2. Divide the class into two groups, A and B, and read the instruction line for each group.
3. Replay scene 2.
4. Instruct each group to complete its exercise.
5. Form pairs, student A with student B. Have students exchange information so that each student's book is complete.
6. Replay scene 2 to review answers.

FURTHER PRACTICE

1. Ask for three student volunteers to take commands from the class.
2. Have the volunteers stand up in the front. The class will dictate commands, one at a time. All three students will perform the action dictated. Repeat with other volunteers.

EXTEND

1. Have the entire class stand up.
2. Replay scene 2 (34:37 to 36:05), and do the exercises along with the video.

RICHARD'S CONDITION

PREPARE

The vocabulary for this exercise appeared in the Act II Preview. You may wish to review it.

PARTICIPATE

1. With the class, read the instruction line and the words for 1–4 and a–d.
2. Play scene 3 (36:06 to 37:14).
3. Have students complete the exercise.
4. Review student answers.
5. Replay the scene to check answers.

YES OR NO?

PREPARE

Pre-teach: *in other words, really, to hurt.*

PARTICIPATE

1. Divide the class into pairs, A and B.
2. With the class, read the instruction line and the questions about Richard and Marilyn.
3. Replay scene 3 (36:06 to 37:14).
4. Have student A ask student B the questions about Richard, and student B ask student A the questions about Marilyn.
5. Review student answers.

EXTEND

1. Discussion: Re-read question 5 about Richard. What does it mean to lie? Hint: Richard doesn't make a false statement to Marilyn, but he avoids telling her the whole situation.
2. Cue the video to 37:09. Play it and pause at 37:11. What does Richard's body language tell you about how he feels?

STORYTELLER

1. Divide the class into small groups.
2. With the class, read the instruction line.
3. Have students complete the exercise. As an alternative, tell students they may tell their group about a situation in their life in which they or someone they know was less than truthful. What happened in the end?

STORYWRITER

1. With the class, read the instruction line.
2. Have students write about Act II or about the situation described in the previous exercise.
3. Give students ten minutes to write.
4. Collect review papers. Select examples to read to the class.

Scene 3: "And your legs don't hurt?"

RICHARD'S CONDITION

SOUND ON
36:06 - 37:14

Watch the scene. How does Richard describe his physical condition? Draw a line between each adjective at the left and the correct noun or noun phrase at the right. The first answer is given.

1. ideal	a. health
2. wonderful	b. blood pressure
3. excellent	c. heart
4. perfect	d. condition

IN PAIRS

YES OR NO?

Watch the scene again. Complete this activity with a partner. Take turns asking and answering the questions. Two answers are given.

About Richard

1. Is Richard tired?
   No, he isn't.
2. Did Richard go to the aerobics class today?
   Yes, he did.
3. Did he exercise?
4. Does Richard tell Marilyn the truth?
5. Does he lie?

About Marilyn

1. Is Marilyn surprised?
2. Does she think Richard attended the class?
3. Does she think he is in good condition?

IN SMALL GROUPS

STORYTELLER

The joke is on Marilyn. Choose one student to retell the story of Act II to the rest of your group. Help him or her to remember the details.

STORYWRITERS

With your group, write the whole story of Act II. Choose one member of your group to be the secretary.

WITH THE WHOLE CLASS

ACT II

PRONUNCIATION

SOUND ON

37:15 - 39:15

Watch the "Focus In" segment twice. The second time, your teacher will pause after each of the following lines. Repeat each line and use the same pronunciation that Jack or Richard uses.

1. **Jack Davis:** *What do you do* for a living, Mr. Stewart?

2. **Jack Davis:** *What do you* photograph?

3. **Richard:** *What do you* mean?

4. **Jack Davis:** *Did you* ever think of photographing an aerobics class?

5. **Jack Davis:** *Don't you* think it'd be a good subject?

6. **Jack Davis:** Maybe *you can* photograph a class . . .

ACT II
INTERMISSION

PRONUNCIATION: *can/can't*

In the "Focus In" activity above, you heard Jack Davis say, "Maybe you can photograph a class . . . ." Jack didn't pronounce the *a* in *can*. Instead, he said *cn*. This is the correct pronunciation of *can* before a verb. But it *is* necessary to pronounce the *a* in the negative form, *can't*. Also, the negative form is stressed (strong), but the positive form is unstressed (weak).

A. Compare the pronunciation of the two sentences in each of the following pairs. Practice saying them.

1. I can type fast. / I can't type fast.
2. She can do it. / She can't do it.
3. We can go tomorrow. / We can't go tomorrow.
4. You can take the bus. / You can't take the bus.

IN PAIRS

B. Complete these two sentences with true information about yourself. Say each sentence to your partner. Then your partner will ask you a question about the information.

1. I know that I can _____
2. I know that I can't _____

FOCUS IN: PRONUNCIATION
PREPARE
Explain to the class that in normal speech, people often take pronunciation short-cuts. Certain sounds are pushed together. Ask the class for examples of this in their native language.

PARTICIPATE
1. With the class, read the instruction line and sentences 1–6.
2. Play the "Focus In" segment (37:15 to 39:15) without pausing.
3. Replay the segment, pausing at the questions. Model the pronunciation if necessary, and ask for individual and chorus repetitions.
4. Repeat as many times as you like.
5. Cue the video to 29:50. Tell students: "The sounds are not always pushed together. Sometimes they are separated for emphasis. Listen:" Play the video (29:50 to 29:59).

   Marilyn: Don't *you* forget.

ACT II INTERMISSION
PRONUNCIATION: *CAN/CAN'T*
PARTICIPATE
1. With the class, read the explanation and instruction line A.
2. Model the pronunciation of examples 1–4, and ask for individual and chorus repetitions.
3. Divide the class into pairs, A and B.
4. With the class, read instruction line B.
5. Have students complete the exercise.
6. Ask for student volunteers to read their examples to the class.

USEFUL LANGUAGE

PREPARE
Read through and explain the expressions to your students.

PARTICIPATE
1. Write the expressions on the board.
2. Initiate the conversation below. Elicit responses from the class. The possible student answers are in parentheses.

Teacher:	You know, my sister-in-law has an interesting job.
Students:	(What does she do for a living?)
Teacher:	She's a wedding planner. She helps people plan their weddings. My hobby is making videos. I have never made a wedding video.
Students:	(Did you ever think of making a wedding video?)
Teacher:	Not really.
Students:	(Don't you think it would be a good subject?)
Teacher:	Sure.
Students:	(How about making a wedding video for your sister-in-law?)
Teacher:	Good idea. You know, I'm getting married soon.
Students:	(Maybe you can make a wedding video for your sister-in-law, and she can plan your wedding.)
Teacher:	Great idea! Why didn't I think of that?

INSTANT ROLE-PLAYS
Repeat the role-play procedure outlined on page 7.

LESSON THREE

ACT III PREVIEW

PREPARE
Pre-teach: *truth, the bet is still on.*

PARTICIPATE
1. With the class, read the instruction line and sentences 1–3.
2. With books closed, play the Preview (39:21 to 39:56).
3. With books open, replay the Preview.
4. Have students complete the exercise.
5. Review correct answers.

EXTEND: WHO'S GOING TO COOK DINNER TONIGHT?
Tell students they'll find out at the end of Act III. *Suggestion:* Make your own bet in class. Losers have to get up and do the exercise routine for the winners.

USEFUL LANGUAGE

In Act II, you heard ways to . . .
- ask about someone's job:
  What do you do for a living?
- make a suggestion:
  Did you ever think of photographing an aerobics class?
  How about today?
- propose a deal:
  Maybe you can photograph a class, and I can give you and Mrs. Stewart a month of classes—free.
- persuade someone:
  Don't you think it'd be a good subject?

IN PAIRS

INSTANT ROLE-PLAYS

Practice these conversations with a partner:

At a party . . .

A: What do you do for a living?
B: I'm an opera singer.
A: That sounds exciting. Do you enjoy traveling?
B: Not really.

At a disco . . .

A: Did you ever think of dancing professionally?
B: Not really.
A: You're very good.
B: Thanks. You are, too.
A: I'm a television producer. Maybe you can teach me to dance, and I can get you on a TV show.

Then complete these conversations:

At a party . . .

A: What do you do for a living?
B: I'm a schoolteacher.
A:
B:

At a gym . . .

A: Did you every think of playing basketball professionally?
B:
A:
B:
A:

ACT III
PREVIEW

SOUND ON

39:21 - 39:56

Watch the preview to complete the sentences. Listen carefully to Richard and Marilyn. Write their words on the blank lines.

1. Richard: _____ exercise.
2. Marilyn: Remember, _____ , _____ entire family.
3. Richard: _____ , _____ entire family.

ACT III
VIDEO GAMES

Scene 1: "Marilyn, I have to tell you something."
UNDERSTUDIES

IN PAIRS

SOUND ON

39:57 - 41:53

Watch the scene and listen to it carefully. Work with a partner to act out the scene. It is not important to repeat Marilyn's and Richard's words exactly. Include the following information:

RICHARD	MARILYN
• says that instead of exercising, he photographed the class	• suggests that they both go to the advanced class at four o'clock
• asks about the bet	• says the bet is still on
	• explains the bet

After you practice the scene, you may perform it for the whole class.

Scene 2: "Don't forget to breathe."
LISTEN IN

SOUND ON

41:54 - 43:19

A. Read each of the words below. Then watch the scene and listen to it carefully. Which of the following words does the instructor use to describe an exercise? Check (☑) only the words you hear.

☐ 1. stretch	☐ 4. jump	☐ 7. pony
☐ 2. skip	☐ 5. twist	☐ 8. hop
☐ 3. scissors	☐ 6. tango	☐ 9. kick

B. Now listen to the scene again to check your answers.

UNDERSTUDIES

PREPARE
Pre-teach: *steak, main course, broccoli, I knew it!, instead of.*

PARTICIPATE
1. Divide the class into pairs, A and B.
2. With the class, read the instruction line and the dialogue that Marilyn and Richard perform in the scene.
3. Ask students to choose a character.
4. Play scene 1 (39:57 to 41:53).
5. Taking the characters one at a time, elicit the dialogue. Allow for variations. Encourage students to use their own ideas. Avoid repeating the actual dialogue word for word. Replay scene 1, if necessary.
6. Have the groups practice the dialogue.
7. Ask for a volunteer group to perform actions and dialogue for the class. Ask for other groups to volunteer. Allow as many groups as wish to volunteer to do so.

LISTEN IN

PREPARE
Pre-teach: *pick up the pace, barely, run it off, finish off, that's it for today.*

PARTICIPATE
1. With the class, read the instruction line and words 1–9 below.
2. Play scene 2 (41:54 to 43:19).
3. Have students complete the exercise on their own.
4. Review student answers.
5. Replay the scene to check answers.

EXTEND
Richard lost the bet. It's time for the losers in the class to get up and do the exercise routine with the video. Use segment 42:36 to 43:15.

WHAT ARE THEY SAYING?

PREPARE

Pre-teach: *thank you but no thank you, huh?, over (finished)*.

PARTICIPATE

1. Divide the class into pairs, A and B.
2. With the class, read the instruction line and the dialogue beneath each photo.
3. Turn the sound off and play scene 3 (43:20 to 44:28).
4. Have students complete the exercise.
5. Replay scene 3, if necessary.
6. Turn the sound on and replay scene 3.
7. Review answers.

FOCUS IN: "HOW MUCH" AND "HOW MANY"

PREPARE

Pre-teach from the Phrase Box: *bunch, loaf* (pl. *loaves*), *head* (of lettuce), *pound, quart*.

PARTICIPATE

1. Divide the class into pairs, A and B.
2. With the class, read the instruction line.
3. Play the "Focus In" segment (44:29 to 46:29).
4. With the class, read the explanation of the use of "much" and "many," and the two-line dialogue.
5. Have students complete the exercise.

EXTEND

If you are planning a class party or outing soon, you may extend the activity by eliciting from the class the different food items and supplies you will need for your party, and the quantities of each.

1. Elicit the food items the class wants to have and write the words on the board.
2. Establish whether each is countable or uncountable.
3. Using the two-line dialogue above, establish the quantity of each needed. Designate a student to direct the exercise.

Scene 3: "Thank you, Jack, but no thank you."

WHAT ARE THEY SAYING?

IN PAIRS

SOUND OFF

43:20 - 44:28

With the sound off, watch the scene. Look for the three scenes in the pictures below. What are the people saying? Circle *a, b,* or *c.*

Richard: a. Is it over already?
b. It was a piece of cake.
c. Marilyn, I'm exhausted. I can't move.

Jack: a. Could you take some more photos?
b. Is this your very first advanced aerobics class?
c. Could you try to raise your knees more next time?

Marilyn: a. I think we'll cook dinner together.
b. Let me show you some more exercises.
c. How did you fall down?

Now, with the sound on, watch the scene to check your answers.

ACT III *Focus In*

"HOW MUCH" AND "HOW MANY"

IN PAIRS

SOUND ON

44:29 - 46:29

Watch the "Focus In" segment. Then complete the activity.

Marilyn asks, "Richard, how much broccoli do I need for seven people?" Use *How much* with uncountable nouns such as *water* and *rice.* Use *How many* with countable nouns such as *apples* and *oranges.* In the scene, Richard doesn't answer Marilyn's question. But he might say, "One bunch should be enough." Ask your partner about each item on the grocery list below. Use *How much* or *How many* in each question. Your partner may answer by using one of the expressions from the Phrase Box.

A: How (*much/many*) _____ do I need for _____ people?
B: _____ should be enough.

broccoli
bread
lettuce
potatoes
steak
ice cream

a *bunch* of broccoli

PHRASE BOX

bunch / bunches of broccoli
loaf / loaves of bread
head / heads of lettuce
pound / pounds of potatoes
pound / pounds of steak
quart / quarts of ice cream

ACT III
FINALE

VOCABULARY AND EXPRESSIONS

Use the words or phrases from the Word and Phrase Box to replace the underlined parts of this summary of Episode 4. On the lines below the summary, rewrite the paragraph and use the new vocabulary from the box.

Marilyn came home from her exercise class, and she felt very tired. She was in a new, more difficult class. Richard laughed and said that her class was very easy. He said that he could exercise in her class. Marilyn didn't think that Richard was in such good physical condition. So Marilyn and Richard made an agreement. The winner had to cook dinner for the whole family.

Richard called Jack Davis, the instructor, to say that he was leaving right away. Everything was arranged. But instead of exercising, Richard made a deal with Jack to photograph the class. Richard arrived home, feeling great, and Marilyn was suprised. Later, Richard told Marilyn the truth, and they decided to go together to a class. They had to turn from side to side, jump on one leg, and do other exercises without resting for an hour. Just when Richard thought he couldn't keep going, the instructor said to go faster. Richard was almost not able to finish.

Marilyn won the bet, but she agreed to cook dinner together with Richard. Marilyn was certainly "a good sport."

<table>
<tr><td>WORD AND PHRASE BOX</td></tr>
<tr><td>pick up the pace</td></tr>
<tr><td>hop</td></tr>
<tr><td>nonstop</td></tr>
<tr><td>on his way over</td></tr>
<tr><td>advanced</td></tr>
<tr><td>aerobics</td></tr>
<tr><td>set</td></tr>
<tr><td>exhausted</td></tr>
<tr><td>a piece of cake</td></tr>
<tr><td>a bet</td></tr>
<tr><td>work out</td></tr>
<tr><td>entire</td></tr>
<tr><td>twist</td></tr>
<tr><td>barely</td></tr>
<tr><td>last</td></tr>
<tr><td>great shape</td></tr>
</table>

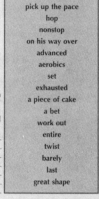

_____
_____
_____
_____
_____
_____
_____
_____
_____
_____
_____
_____
_____
_____

ACT III FINALE
VOCABULARY AND EXPRESSIONS

PREPARE
With the class, review the words and expressions in the Word and Phrase Box.

PARTICIPATE
1. With the class, read the instruction line and the summary. You may wish to do all or part of the summary as a dictation exercise.
2. Have students complete the exercise.
3. Review answers.

USEFUL LANGUAGE

PREPARE

Read through and explain the expressions to your students.

PARTICIPATE

1. Have students close their books.
2. Make the statements below. Elicit responses from the class. The possible student answers are in parentheses.

Teacher:	Someone wants to know if you would like to stand up and exercise again. What would you say?
Student:	(Thank you but no thank you.)
Teacher:	Somebody plays a joke on you. What do you say to them?
Student:	(Just wait.)
Teacher:	You told me to pick up some bread for you at the store. I'm leaving now. Remind me.
Student:	(Don't forget to pick up the bread.)
Teacher:	Someone's book is different than yours. It has all the answers in it. What do you say to that person?
Student:	(I knew it!)
Teacher:	Suppose you played a joke on me. Now you want to tell me the truth. How do you begin?
Student:	(I have something to tell you. *or* I have to tell you something.)

INSTANT ROLE-PLAYS

PREPARE

Pre-teach: *speeding ticket, to act crazy, 35-mile zone.*

PARTICIPATE

Repeat the role-play procedure outlined on page 7.

U.S. LIFE

PREPARE

Pre-teach: *pulse, chest x-ray.*

PARTICIPATE

1. Have students read independently.
2. Ask: "What things does a doctor check in a complete physical examination?"

YOUR TURN

Complete this exercise in small groups or with the entire class.

USEFUL LANGUAGE

In Act III, you heard ways to . . .

- introduce an explanation:
  I have to tell you something.
  (or: *I have something to tell you.*)
- react to news you expected:
  I knew it!

- remind someone:
  Remember . . .
  Don't forget to . . .
- say you're enjoying something:
  This is fun.

- threaten or warn someone:
  Just wait.
- refuse an offer:
  Thank you . . . but no thank you.
- say something is finished:
  That's it for today.

IN PAIRS

INSTANT ROLE-PLAYS

Practice this conversation with a partner:

At home, after the party . . .

Son:	Mom, I have to tell you something.
Mom:	Yes, what is it?
Son:	I got a speeding ticket when I was driving your car.
Mom:	I knew it! You act crazy when you're out late with your friends.
Son:	I'm sorry. I was only going 40 miles an hour in a 35-mile zone.
Mom:	Well, that's it for this month. No more driving for you!
Son:	I know.
Mom:	Just wait until your father hears about this. He'll be upset.
Son:	I promise I won't do it again.

Then complete this conversation:

At home, at the end of the school term . . .

Daughter:	Dad, I have something to tell you.
Dad:	Yes, what is it?
Daughter:	I got a "D" in my European history class.
Dad:	
Daughter:	
Dad:	
Daughter:	
Dad:	
Daughter:	

READ AND DISCUSS

Read the paragraph under "U.S. Life." Then discuss your answers to the questions under "Your Turn."

ON YOUR OWN

U.S. LIFE

Many Americans see their doctor once a year for a **complete physical**, or checkup. During a complete physical examination, the doctor checks the patient's pulse and blood pressure. In addition, he may order blood tests and a chest X-ray. When the results of these tests are completed, the doctor gives the patient a report on his or her general health. The doctor may also recommend a **fitness program** (a diet or exercise) for good health.

IN SMALL GROUPS

YOUR TURN

1. When was your last complete physical?
2. Describe the perfect fitness program for you.

EPISODE 5
"The Right Magic"

In this unit, you will practice . . .

making suggestions
talking about the weather
describing a sequence

ACT I
PREVIEW

SOUND ON

1:00 - 1:46

Watch the preview to complete the sentences. Choose the correct words from the Word Box. Write the words on the blank lines. The first answer is given.

WORD BOX

am

pretty

could

Maybe

planning

guess

has

fishing

game

these

busy

1. **Robbie:** Dad and I were _planning_ to go to the _____, but he _____ to work today.

2. **Grandpa:** _____ your dad and I _____ take you _____ with us.

3. **Robbie:** But Dad is always so _____.

4. **Grandpa:** You're working _____ hard _____ days.

5. **Philip:** I _____ I _____.

What does Philip decide to do?

EPISODE 5: "The Right Magic"

SUMMARY
Grandpa, Philip, and Robbie go fishing.

LANGUAGE
• making suggestions
• talking about the weather
• describing a sequence

U.S. LIFE
• leisure activities
• superstitions

ADVANCE PLANNING
1. Bring to class some string and a hat as props for the UNDERSTUDIES exercise in Act II.
2. Ask students to think about a situation in their lives when someone helped them in an emergency. They will tell the class about it in Act III.
3. Bring to class some good luck charms to discuss at the end of Act III.

LESSON ONE

ACT I PREVIEW

PARTICIPATE
1. With the class, read the instruction line, the words beneath the photos, and the words in the Word Box.
2. Have students watch the entire Preview without writing.
3. Play the Preview (1:00 to 1:46).
4. Have students complete the exercise.
5. Play the Preview again so students can review their answers.

EXTEND: WHAT DOES PHILIP DECIDE TO DO?
Discuss: Focus on Grandpa. What role do you think he's going to play in this episode?

LISTEN IN

PREPARE

Pre-teach: *to hand* (give) *something, refrigerator, fried eggs, bacon, cloudy, warm, sunny, computer, program, to work at* (learn) *something.*

PARTICIPATE

1. With the class, read the instruction line and statements 1–9 below.
2. Play scene 1 (1:47 to 3:37).
3. Have students complete the exercise on their own.
4. Review student answers.
5. Replay the scene to check answers.

SPLIT DIALOGUE

PREPARE

Pre-teach: *ward* (of a hospital).

PARTICIPATE

1. Divide the class into pairs, A and B.
2. With the class, read the instruction line and the words in the Word Box.
3. Ask students to choose a character, Grandpa or Philip, and listen carefully to what their character says.
4. With books closed, play scene 2 (3:38 to 4:06).
5. With books open, replay scene 2. Instruct students to follow in their books.
6. Have students complete the exercise.
7. Replay scene 2, if necessary.
8. Review student answers.

ACT I
VIDEO GAMES

Scene 1: "But Dad is always so busy."

LISTEN IN

SOUND ON

1:47 - 3:37

Read the statements below. Then watch the scene and listen to it carefully. Which of the following items are true according to the information in the scene? Put a check (✔) in the box only if you are sure the sentence is true.

☐ 1. Grandpa made a lot of bacon for breakfast.

☐ 2. Robbie plays baseball.

☐ 3. The weather is good today.

☐ 4. Philip has to work today.

☐ 5. Grandpa played baseball when he was young.

☐ 6. In school, Robbie is having problems with math.

☐ 7. Robbie has a new math program for his computer.

☐ 8. Grandpa has never used a computer before.

☐ 9. Robbie is not busy tomorrow.

Scene 2: "You're working pretty hard these days."

SPLIT DIALOGUE

IN PAIRS

SOUND ON

3:38 - 4:06

Watch the scene. Fill in each blank with the correct *verb* or *auxiliary* from the Word Box. Work with a partner. One of you will complete Grandpa's lines; the other will complete Philip's. Play the scene as many times as necessary.

GRANDPA

1. Robbie _____ you
   _____
   him to the game today.

2. I _____ .

3. Definitely. We _____ .
   You and Robbie and me. _____
   our first fishing trip?

Now watch the scene again. Check your answers with your partner. Then practice reading the dialogue together.

WORD BOX

understand
feel
spend
says
need
take
Remember
See
can
can't
should

PHILIP

1. I really _____ bad about it, but they
   _____ me at the hospital today, in the
   children's ward.

2. Maybe we _____
   some time together next weekend.

3. I sure do. . . . Well, I've got to run, Dad,
   _____ you later.

Scene 3: *"It'll be like old times . . ."*
ON THE PATIO

PREPARE

1. Pre-teach: *to think about something* (to consider doing something), *to catch* (fish), *paper work, thrilled, it'll be like old times, what's the weather going to be like?, sunny and mild, don't thank me* (don't mention it).

2. CULTURE NOTE: Fishing is one of the activities in America which has traditionally been a special father–son activity.

IN PAIRS

SOUND ON

4:07 - 6:01

Watch the scene and listen to it carefully. Then work with a partner to ask and answer the following questions.

1. When is Robbie's birthday?
2. When did Philip and Robbie last go fishing together?
3. How many fish did they catch?
4. What happened the first time Philip and Grandpa went fishing together?
5. What type of work was Philip planning to do tomorrow?
6. What's the weather going to be like?

PARTICIPATE

1. Divide the class into pairs, A and B.
2. With the class, read the instruction line and questions 1–6.
3. Play scene 3 (4:07 to 6:01).
4. Have student A ask student B questions 1–3, and student B ask student A questions 4–6.
5. Replay the segment, if necessary.
6. Review student answers.

EXTEND

Discuss: Why does Philip thank Grandpa?

1. Write this on the board:
   Philip: "Thanks for _____
   _____."

2. Replay segment 5:39 to 5:50.
3. Ask students to complete the sentence on the board.
4. Discuss student answers.

HOW DOES GRANDPA FEEL?

WITH THE WHOLE CLASS

SOUND ON

1:47 - 6:01

Read the three possible explanations of Grandpa's feelings in Act I. Which paragraph best describes his feelings? Circle A, B, or C. Explain your choice. If you wish, you may watch Act I again to find the answer.

A
Grandpa is lonely. He wants someone in the family to spend more time with him. So he asks Robbie to teach him how to use the computer. He also wants Philip and Robbie to spend time with him next weekend.

B
Grandpa is concerned that his son Philip is not able to spend time with the family. He wants Philip to relax more and enjoy life. He wants Philip to share with Robbie some of the experiences he and Philip shared when Philip was growing up.

C
Grandpa is worried about getting old. He wants to learn about new things, such as how to use a computer. He also wants to do some of the things he did when he was younger, such as go fishing.

PREPARE

1. Pre-teach: *lonely, to relax, to share experiences*.
2. Write the letters

   A   B   C

   across the board.

PARTICIPATE

1. With the class, read the instruction line and paragraphs A, B, and C below.
2. Replay Act I (1:47 to 6:01).
3. For each paragraph, elicit examples of Grandpa's dialogue or actions in Act I that support that paragraph as being the correct one. Write notes under A, B, and C. Ask students: "What did Grandpa say or do to make you think A is the best explanation?"
4. Arrive at a consensus with your class as to the best explanation, A, B, or C.

FOCUS IN: WEATHER

PREPARE

1. Using a map of the United States or the map provided in the text, review the major cities and geographical regions of the United States.
2. Pre-teach: *skyscraper, surrounding area, gorgeous, popular vacation spot, Fahrenheit °F, Celsius °C, gateway, cool, windy, to expect, throughout, freezing, snow*.

PARTICIPATE

1. With the class, read instruction line A.
2. With books closed, play the "Focus In" segment (6:02 to 8:01).
3. With books open, replay the "Focus In" segment. Have students complete exercise A only.
4. Review student answers.
5. With the class, read instruction line B.
6. Replay the "Focus In" segment, question by question. You may wish to repeat a question before going on. The times are:
   a. 6:21 to 6:38.
   b. 6:39 to 7:01.
   c. 7:02 to 7:17.
   d. 7:18 to 7:39.
   e. 7:40 to 7:54.
7. Review student answers.

ACT 1
WEATHER

SOUND ON

6:02 - 8:01

A. Watch the "Focus In" segment. Then answer the questions below. Circle the letter of each correct answer.

1. Which city will be very hot?
   a. New York b. Miami c. St. Louis d. Denver e. Los Angeles
2. Which city will be very cold?
   a. New York b. Miami c. St. Louis d. Denver e. Los Angeles
3. Which city will have rain?
   a. New York b. Miami c. St. Louis d. Denver e. Los Angeles
4. Which city will be windy?
   a. New York b. Miami c. St. Louis d. Denver e. Los Angeles
5. Which city will have snow?
   a. New York b. Miami c. St. Louis d. Denver e. Los Angeles

B. Watch the "Focus In" segment again. <u>Underline</u> the words you hear about each city or area. The answers for *New York City* are given.

1. New York City:	<u>Statue of Liberty</u> <u>mild</u>	subway <u>cloudy</u>	<u>skyscrapers</u> <u>warm</u>	<u>sunny</u> <u>fishing</u>
2. the Southeast:	gorgeous hot	Miami Fahrenheit	vacation Celsius	sport beach
3. St. Louis:	gateway windy	West rain	cool highway	school Midwest
4. the Rocky Mountains:	freezing Colorado	cold temperature	outside snow	Denver skiing
5. the West Coast:	Las Vegas ocean	Los Angeles Disneyland	California drive	cars coast

IN SMALL GROUPS

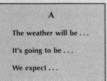

C. What is the weather going to be like in other places? Choose some cities you know and give a *weather forecast*, a report about the weather in the near future. Use words or phrases from each box below.

A	B		C
The weather will be . . .	sunny	mild	It'll be a beautiful day to . . .
It's going to be . . .	cloudy	warm	It'll be a perfect day for . . .
	cool	windy	It'll be a perfect place for . . .
We expect . . .	freezing	rain(ing)	
	degrees	snow(ing)	
	Fahrenheit	Celsius	

ACT I
INTERMISSION
GRAMMAR AND EXPRESSIONS:

IN PAIRS

Negative *yes/no* Questions

This morning, Philip told Grandpa about his plans to work at the hospital tomorrow. But now Philip says he can go fishing tomorrow. So Grandpa has a reason to believe that Philip *doesn't* have to work tomorrow. Grandpa asks, "Don't you have to work?"

Philip has to work tomorrow. But now he's talking about going fishing tomorrow.

Don't you have to work?

Ask a negative *yes/no* question when you *thought* that something was true, *but now* you have a reason not to be sure.

Compare

Do you have to work? (I don't know the answer.)
Don't you have to work? (I thought the answer was *yes*. But now I'm not sure.)

Write a negative *yes/no* question for each situation below. Use the <u>underlined</u> information in your question. The first answer is given.

1. Your friend bought tickets for a baseball game today. You thought, "He's going to the game." But now your friend says he will watch TV all day. You ask, ***"Aren't you going to the game?"***

2. Your friend has a computer in his office. You thought, <u>"He knows how to use the computer."</u> But now your friend says he always uses a typewriter to write letters. You ask, " _____

3. Your friend called to tell you to get ready for a delicious fish dinner. She was fishing all day. You thought, <u>"She caught a lot of fish."</u> But now she comes home and suggests going out to a restaurant for dinner. You ask, "_____ "

4. You heard the weather forecaster on the radio say, <u>"It's going to rain today."</u> But now your friend says he will go to the beach. You ask, "_____ "

EXTEND

1. Divide the class into small groups. You may wish to group students who share knowledge of a specific country or city.
2. With the class, read the instruction line and review the expressions in the boxes.
3. Have each group of students select a city or region noted for its weather, either good or bad.
4. Have students make up a weather forecast about their selected region or city, using one expression from each of the boxes, and in the same order as the boxes.
5. Ask for volunteers to read their forecasts.

ACT I INTERMISSION
GRAMMAR AND EXPRESSIONS

PARTICIPATE

1. Divide the class into pairs, A and B.
2. With the class, read the explanation and examples and sentences 1–4 below.
3. Have students complete the exercise.

FURTHER PRACTICE

1. Write these negative question openers on the board: Don't . . . ? Can't . . . ? Aren't . . . ?
     Weren't . . . ? Didn't . . . ?
2. Make the statements below to the class to elicit negative questions such as in the example. Encourage multiple answers and variations. Tell students to start their questions with one of the expressions on the board.

Teacher:	You know, I have to walk home from school today.
Student:	(Don't you have a car? Don't you have money for the bus/subway? etc.)
Teacher:	I'm not going to eat much for lunch today.
	I didn't watch TV last week.
	I never go into the water at the beach.
	My life is perfect right now.
	I never plan to get married.
	I stayed up all night last night reading.

Note: If students have difficulty forming a question, make a statement and point to the question word, on the board, you want them to use.

USEFUL LANGUAGE

PREPARE
Read through and explain the expressions to your students.

PARTICIPATE
1. Have students close their books.
2. Make the statements below. Elicit responses from the class. The possible student answers are in parentheses.

Teacher: I'm hungry.

Student: (How about something to eat? *or* Maybe we should get something to eat now. *or* Can you have lunch with me?)

Teacher: What's the weather going to be like tomorrow?

Student: (Answers will vary.)

Teacher: What are some things you can do on a picnic in the park?

Student: (Activities with *go*.)

Teacher: We used to go camping all the time.

Student: (Maybe we should do it again.)

Teacher: Ok. Let's go. Will it be fun?

Student: (It will be like old times.)

INSTANT ROLE-PLAYS

PREPARE
Pre-teach: *leaky faucet, wrench*.

PARTICIPATE
Repeat the role-play procedure outlined on page 7.

USEFUL LANGUAGE

In Act I, you heard ways to . . .

• ask for an object:
 Hand me two eggs.

• make suggestions:
 How about some bacon?
 Maybe you can teach me how to work on a computer someday.
 Can you come fishing with me tomorrow?
 Maybe we should do it again.

• talk about the weather:
 It's a perfect day . . . a little cloudy but nice and warm.
 [The] radio says [it'll be] sunny and mild.

• talk about activities with go:
 go fishing (also: *go bowling, go shopping, go running, go swimming, go dancing*)

• say you're in a hurry and must leave:
 I've got to run.

• check information you thought you knew:
 Don't you have to work?

• remember the past:
 It'll be like old times.

IN PAIRS

INSTANT ROLE-PLAYS

Practice these conversations with a partner:

Saturday afternoon at home . . .

A: Aren't you going bowling with Henry this afternoon?
B: No. I really feel bad about it, but I have to fix this leaky faucet.
A: Hand me the wrench, and I'll fix it for you.
B: Thanks! But aren't you going swimming today?
A: No. The radio says it'll rain, so I'm staying home.
B: Thanks for your help.
A: Don't thank me. I love working around the house.

Then complete these conversations:

Saturday afternoon at the college dormitory . . .

A: Aren't you going to the big football game this afternoon?
B:

A:
B:
A:
B:
A:

On the way to the beach resort . . .

Wife: When did we last visit this resort?
Husband: I remember exactly. It was on our fifth wedding anniversary, three years ago.
Wife: Maybe we can swim at that white sand beach again.
Husband: Great idea! It'll be just like old times.
Wife: The children will be thrilled.
Husband: Me, too.

On the way to the cabin in the woods . . .

A: When did we last go up to the cabin?
B:

A:

B:
A:
B:

WHAT IS HE SAYING?

PREPARE
Pre-teach: *rare, medium, well-done, burned, help!* (distress call), *easy does it, to breathe.*

PARTICIPATE
1. With the class, read the instruction line and the words beneath the photos.
2. Turn the sound off and play scene 3 (12:24 to 13:34).
3. Have students complete the exercise.
4. Turn the sound on and play scene 3 again.
5. Review student answers.

FREEZE!

PARTICIPATE
1. Pre-teach: *to drown, mouth to mouth resuscitation, to survive.*
2. Ask the class:
   Does Albert know how to swim?
   Does Robbie?
   How long was Albert in the water?
   What is Philip doing to save his life?

FOCUS IN: DESCRIBING A SEQUENCE

PREPARE
1. Pre-teach these time expressions and write them on the board: *first, next, then, after that, later on, finally, last.*
2. To introduce your class to the concept of describing a sequence, mime a sequence of actions in the classroom for them. Have students watch you carefully and remember your actions.
   a. Open the door.
   b. Look outside.
   c. Close the door.
3. Using the cue words on the board, ask students to tell you the sequence:
   First, you opened the door.
   Then, you looked outside.
   Last, you closed the door.
4. Mime a sequence of five classroom actions and elicit the sequence from your students using the cue words *first, next, after that, later on, finally.*

PARTICIPATE
Watch the "Focus In" segment (13:35 to 15:36).

STORYTELLER
1. Divide the class into small groups.
2. With the class, read the instruction line.
3. Have students choose a member of their group to retell the story.

STORYWRITER
1. With the class, read the instruction line.
2. Have students complete the exercise.

Scene 3: "Breathe, Albert!"

WHAT IS HE SAYING?

SOUND OFF

12:24 - 13:34

With the sound off, watch the scene. Look for the three scenes in the pictures below. What is Philip saying? Circle a, b, or c.

Philip: a. Do you like your fish rare, medium, or well done?
b. I hope you like your fish well done.
c. I'm sorry I burned this fish.

Philip: a. Easy does it, Robbie.
b. Never mind, Robbie. I can do it alone.
c. Help me lift him out of the water, Son.

Philip: a. Robbie, find his father right now!
b. Robbie, call an ambulance right away!
c. Robbie, run to the car! Bring a blanket and my medical bag.

Now, with the sound on, watch the scene to check your answers.

FREEZE!

WITH THE WHOLE CLASS

PAUSE AT 13:34

Will Albert survive? Tell your opinions. You will find out the answer in Act III!

IN SMALL GROUPS

ACT II
DESCRIBING A SEQUENCE

SOUND ON

13:35 - 15:36

Watch the "Focus In" segment. Then do the activities below.

STORYTELLER
Choose one student from your group to retell the story of Act II to the rest of the class. Help him or her to remember the details. Use the words and expressions from the Word Box.

WORD BOX
First . . .
Next . . .
Then . . .
After that . . .
Later on . . .
Finally . . .
Last . . .

STORYWRITERS
With your group, write the whole story of Act II. Choose one member of your group to be the secretary. Use the words and expressions from the Word Box.

READ AND DISCUSS

Read the paragraphs under "U.S. Life." Then discuss your answers to the questions under "Your Turn."

ON YOUR OWN

U.S. LIFE
More than fifty years ago, at the New York World's Fair, the forecast for American life was something like this: "In the future, technology will bring a higher **standard of living.** Labor-saving machines will give Americans more free time."

But this forecast was only partly true. Modern machines, like Robbie's home computer, make work simpler, but life is also more complicated. In many American families, both the husband and wife have jobs. This gives them less free time. Like Philip, many Americans have trouble finding time for personal activities such as fishing. But most Americans are able to enjoy some **leisure time.** Because they are so busy, many Americans need to plan their leisure time carefully.

IN SMALL GROUPS

YOUR TURN
1. How many hours of leisure time do you have each week?
2. What are your favorite leisure activities?

ACT II
PREVIEW

SOUND ON

8:07 - 8:44

Watch the preview to complete the sentences. Choose the correct words from the Word Box. Write the words on the blank lines.

1.

Coming up in Act II, Grandpa, Philip, and Robbie _____ fishing.

2.

A young boy _____ Albert is fishing, too. But he's _____

WORD BOX
teaches
alone
go
got
named
trouble
send
lucky
magic

3.

Grandpa _____ Robbie his fisherman's _____
"Fish, fish, _____ me a fish."

4.

And Robbie gets _____.
"I _____ one."
But later, there's _____

U.S. LIFE

PREPARE
Pre-teach: *forecast, technology, standard of living, labor-saving machines, leisure time.*

PARTICIPATE
1. Have students read independently.
2. Ask for volunteers to read aloud.
3. Ask this comprehension question:
   In what two ways is American life different from the forecast of fifty years ago?

YOUR TURN
Complete this exercise in small groups or with the entire class.

LESSON TWO

ACT II PREVIEW

PREPARE
Pre-teach: *magic, to get lucky.*

PARTICIPATE
1. With the class, read the instruction line and the words beneath the photos. Review the words in the Word Box.
2. With books closed, play the Preview (8:07 to 8:44).
3. Have students complete the exercise.
4. Replay the preview if necessary.
5. Review student answers.

LISTEN IN

PREPARE

Pre-teach: *neat* (informal for "good," "great"), *in order to, here we go, not a chance, to watch someone* (guard someone from harm).

PARTICIPATE

1. With the class, read the instruction line and statements 1–12 below.
2. Play scene 1 (8:45 to 10:36).
3. Have students complete the exercise on their own.
4. Review student answers.
5. Replay the scene to check answers.

THE SUBTEXT

PARTICIPATE

1. With the class, read the thought bubbles around the photo and the instruction line.
2. Replay scene 1 (8:45 to 10:36). Students may ask you to pause in several different places for the same answer. Ask the student what Robbie, Philip, or Grandpa said. Then go on. Answers may vary. Encourage students to explain their answers.

EXTEND

Students will have a good idea of what is going to happen in this episode. Ask students what they think each of the characters will do.

What will Albert do?

What will Philip do?

Robbie? Grandpa?

ACT II
VIDEO GAMES

Scene 1: "I just saw a big one!"

LISTEN IN

SOUND ON

8:45 - 10:36

Read the statements below. Then watch the scene and listen to it carefully. Which of the following items are true according to the information in the scene? Put a check (✓) in the box only if you are sure the sentence is true.

- [ ] 1. Robbie is hungry.
- [ ] 2. Philip has fished in this lake before.
- [ ] 3. Grandpa taught Philip how to fish.
- [ ] 4. There are big fish in this lake.
- [ ] 5. Albert is ten years old.
- [ ] 6. Albert is on vacation.
- [ ] 7. Albert's father is at the lodge.
- [ ] 8. Albert doesn't know how to swim.
- [ ] 9. Philip is worried about Albert.
- [ ] 10. The water in the lake is deep.
- [ ] 11. Albert is not a good fisherman.
- [ ] 12. It is going to rain soon.

WITH THE WHOLE CLASS

THE SUBTEXT

1 *Robbie: I'm hungry.*

2 *Philip: I'm afraid he might fall into the water.*

3 *Grandpa: Shouldn't you be here with an adult?*

Read Philip's, Grandpa's, and Robbie's thoughts above. Then watch the scene again and listen to the men's conversation. What do the characters say to express these thoughts? Tell your teacher to stop the tape when you hear each answer.

Scene 2: "See, it works!"

WHAT'S GOING ON?

IN SMALL GROUPS

SOUND ON
PICTURE OFF

10:37 - 12:23

With the picture off, listen to the scene. Try to guess the action. Read each paragraph below. With your group, choose the correct story. Circle the number of your group's choice.

1. Grandpa tells Robbie his magic way to catch a fish. When he turns his hat around, it drops into the water. Robbie repeats the magic words and catches a fish. With his fishing rod, Philip is able to get Grandpa's hat out of the water. The men decide to build a fire to dry the hat. They ask Albert to join them, but he wants to keep fishing.

2. Grandpa tells Robbie his magic way to catch a fish. Robbie repeats the magic words and catches a big fish. Grandpa can't get Robbie's fish into the net, but then Philip catches a fish. The men decide to build a fire to cook the fish for lunch. They ask Albert to join them, but he wants to keep fishing.

3. Grandpa tells Robbie his magic way to catch a fish. Robbie repeats the magic words and catches a big fish. Philip feels something on his fishing line, too. But when he pulls it out of the water, there is a boot on the line. The men ask Albert to help them build a fire, but he wants to keep fishing.

Now, with the picture on, watch the scene to check your answer.

UNDERSTUDIES

IN GROUPS OF THREE

SOUND ON

10:37 - 12:23

Watch the scene again and listen to it carefully. Work in groups of three to act out the scene. It is not important to repeat Grandpa's, Philip's, and Robbie's words exactly. Include the following information:

GRANDPA	PHILIP	ROBBIE
• teaches Robbie his magic way to catch a fish	• tells Robbie he wants to catch his lunch, not buy it	• says he wants to buy lunch
• says the magic words	• asks Grandpa to say the magic words	• repeats the magic words
	• catches a boot	• feels a fish on the line
	• invites Albert to help them build a fire for cooking	• asks Grandpa to get the net
		• tells Philip that Philip forgot to say the magic words

After you practice the scene, you may perform it for the whole class.

WHAT'S GOING ON?

PREPARE

Pre-teach: *fishing line, fishing net, boot.*

PARTICIPATE

1. With the class, read the instruction line and paragraphs 1–3.
2. Turn the picture off and play scene 2 (10:37 to 12:23).
3. Have students complete the exercise.
4. Turn the picture on and play scene 2 again.
5. Review student answers.

UNDERSTUDIES

PREPARE

1. Pre-teach: *It works* (It's effective), *You bet* (You're right).
2. Assemble the following props: three pointers or rulers and some string as fishing poles, a hat, a paper fish, a boot or shoe.

PARTICIPATE

1. Divide the class into groups of three, A, B, and C.
2. With the class, read the instruction line and the actions that Grandpa, Philip, and Robbie perform in the scene.
3. Ask students to choose a character.
4. Play scene 2 again.
5. Taking the characters one at a time, elicit the dialogue. Allow for variations. Encourage students to use their own ideas. Avoid repeating the actual dialogue word for word. Replay scene 2, if necessary.
6. Have the groups practice the dialogue.
7. Ask for a volunteer group to perform the scene for the class. Ask for other groups to volunteer. Allow as many groups as wish to volunteer to do so.

EXTEND

1. Write this scene change on the board: Philip hooks a car tire and falls in the water. Then Ellen, Marilyn, and Susan arrive.
2. Organize groups of three to play Ellen, Marilyn, and Susan.
3. Seat the new groups and the old groups together to work out new dialogue. Hint: Maybe the women have had better luck fishing.
4. Ask for volunteers to act the new scene in front of the class.

ACT II
INTERMISSION

USEFUL LANGUAGE

In Act II, you heard ways to . . .

- correct someone in a joking way:
  Burned, you mean.
- say you're starting to do something:
  Here we go.

- greet someone informally:
  Hi, there!
- say *no* emphatically:
  Not a chance!
  No way!

- tell someone to do something slowly and carefully
  Easy does it.
- encourage someone:
  That's it.
  Come on.
  That a boy/girl.

IN PAIRS

↕ **INSTANT ROLE-PLAYS**

Practice this conversation with a partner.

After falling on the ski slope . . .

A: Hi, there! Can I help you?
B: Thanks. I can't get myself up.
A: Easy does it. That a boy/girl.
B: Thank you.
A: This is an exciting hill, isn't it?
B: Dangerous, you mean.
A: Would you like to follow me down?
B: Down the steep way?
A: Sure. Come on.
B: Not a chance!
A: Don't worry. I'll go slowly.
B: Well, OK.
A: Here we go . . .

Then complete this conversation:

After playing 18 holes of golf . . .

A: Well, that was fun.
B:
A: Want to play another nine holes?
B:
A:
B:
A:
B:
A:
B:
A:
B:
A:

ACT III
PREVIEW

IN PAIRS

SOUND ON

15:43 - 16:16

Watch the preview. With your partner, take turns asking and answering the following questions. Answer *yes, no,* or *We'll wait and see.*

1. Does Philip find Albert's father at the lodge?
2. Does Philip take Albert to the hospital?
3. Does Grandpa want to continue fishing?
4. Does Philip go back to the car to get a jacket?
5. Does Philip receive a call from the hospital?
6. Will Robbie be disappointed?

ACT II INTERMISSION
USEFUL LANGUAGE

PREPARE
Read through and explain the expressions to your students.

PARTICIPATE
1. Have students close their books.
2. Make the statements below. Elicit responses from the class. The possible student answers are in parentheses.

Teacher: Look. I'm carrying a stack of expensive dishes.
Student: (Easy does it.)
Teacher: Shall we have a test today?
Student: (No way! *or* Not a chance!)
Teacher: Look! There goes a friend of yours. Get his attention.
Student: (Hi, there!)
Teacher: I'm your son/daughter. I just got an A on my history exam.
Student: (That a boy/girl.)
Teacher: My book is different than yours. It has all the answers in it.
Student: (I knew it!)
Teacher: Let's drive the car real fast. It will be *fun.*
Student: (Dangerous, you mean.)

INSTANT ROLE-PLAYS

PREPARE
Pre-teach: *steep, nine holes* (of golf).

PARTICIPATE
Repeat the role-play procedure outlined on page 7.

LESSON THREE

ACT III PREVIEW

PREPARE
Pre-teach: *suggestion, beeper* (portable, remote call device usually carried by doctors so that they can be called in case of an emergency).

PARTICIPATE
1. Divide the class into pairs, A and B.
2. With the class, read the instruction line and questions 1–6.
3. Play the Preview (15:43 to 16:16).
4. Have students complete the exercise.
5. Review correct answers.

EXTEND: HOW WILL ROBBIE FEEL?
1. Pre-teach and write on the board:

   easy-going   rigid

2. Ask students: What kind of person is Robbie?
3. Discuss: How do you react when your plans are changed suddenly?

MAKE A MATCH

PREPARE

1. Pre-teach: *uh-oh, grateful, what do you say we . . .* (as suggestion opener).
2. Divide the class into two groups, A and B.

PARTICIPATE

1. Turn the sound off and play scene 1 (16:17 to 18:07).
2. With group A, read the instruction line and numbers 1–4 in the Group A box at the left. Have group A complete the exercise.
3. With group B, read the instruction line and the dialogues in the Group B box at the right. Have group B complete the exercise.
4. Form pairs, student A with student B.
5. Turn the sound on and replay scene 1.
6. Have students number the photos in the correct order.
7. Review the correct order with the students.

FURTHER PRACTICE

Have pairs practice the dialogue for each picture.

EXTEND

Discuss: Ask students to think of a time someone helped them in an emergency, or a time they helped someone. What did they say to the person who helped them?

ACT III
VIDEO GAMES
Scene 1: "Your dad is quite a guy."

IN TWO GROUPS

MAKE A MATCH

SOUND OFF
16:17 - 18:07

With the sound off, watch the video. Then follow the instructions for your group.

GROUP A

Match each sentence below with one of the pictures. Write the number of the correct sentence in the circle at the top left of each picture.

1. Albert's father thanks Robbie for pulling his son from the lake.
2. Grandpa suggests getting back to their fishing.
3. Philip takes Albert to his father.
4. Philip gets a call from the hospital.

GROUP B

Match each of the four pieces of dialogue below with one of the pictures. Write the letter of the correct dialogue in the box at the top right of each picture.

a. **Philip:** Uh-oh. It's probably the hospital. I have to get to a phone.
b. **Father:** I'm very grateful, Robbie.
c. **Grandpa:** Well, what do you say we get back to our fishing?
   Philip: That's a great idea.
d. **Albert:** I want my daddy!
   Philip: We'll take you to him.

IN PAIRS

With the sound on, watch the scene again. Check your work with a partner from the other group. Then say the four pieces of dialogue above in the correct order.

READ AND DISCUSS

Read the paragraphs under "U.S. Life." Then discuss your answers to the questions under "Your Turn."
ON YOUR OWN

U.S. LIFE

More than fifty years ago, at the New York World's Fair, the forecast for American life was something like this: "In the future, technology will bring a higher **standard of living**. Labor-saving machines will give Americans more free time."

But this forecast was only partly true. Modern machines, like Robbie's home computer, make work simpler, but life is also more complicated. In many American families, both the husband and wife have jobs. This gives them less free time. Like Philip, many Americans have trouble finding time for personal activities such as fishing. But most Americans are able to enjoy some **leisure time**. Because they are so busy, many Americans need to plan their leisure time carefully.

IN SMALL GROUPS

YOUR TURN
1. How many hours of leisure time do you have each week?
2. What are your favorite leisure activities?

ACT II
PREVIEW

SOUND ON

8:07 - 8:44

Watch the preview to complete the sentences. Choose the correct words from the Word Box. Write the words on the blank lines.

1.

Coming up in Act II, Grandpa, Philip, and Robbie _____ fishing.

WORD BOX
teaches
alone
go
got
named
trouble
send
lucky
magic

2.

A young boy _____ Albert is fishing, too. But he's _____.

3.

Grandpa _____ Robbie his fisherman's _____.
"Fish, fish, _____ me a fish."

4.

And Robbie gets _____.
"I _____ one."
But later, there's _____.

U.S. LIFE

PREPARE
Pre-teach: *forecast, technology, standard of living, labor-saving machines, leisure time.*

PARTICIPATE
1. Have students read independently.
2. Ask for volunteers to read aloud.
3. Ask this comprehension question:
   In what two ways is American life different from the forecast of fifty years ago?

YOUR TURN
Complete this exercise in small groups or with the entire class.

LESSON TWO

ACT II PREVIEW

PREPARE
Pre-teach: *magic, to get lucky.*

PARTICIPATE
1. With the class, read the instruction line and the words beneath the photos. Review the words in the Word Box.
2. With books closed, play the Preview (8:07 to 8:44).
3. Have students complete the exercise.
4. Replay the preview if necessary.
5. Review student answers.

LISTEN IN

PREPARE

Pre-teach: *neat* (informal for "good," "great"), *in order to, here we go, not a chance, to watch someone* (guard someone from harm).

PARTICIPATE

1. With the class, read the instruction line and statements 1–12 below.
2. Play scene 1 (8:45 to 10:36).
3. Have students complete the exercise on their own.
4. Review student answers.
5. Replay the scene to check answers.

THE SUBTEXT

PARTICIPATE

1. With the class, read the thought bubbles around the photo and the instruction line.
2. Replay scene 1 (8:45 to 10:36). Students may ask you to pause in several different places for the same answer. Ask the student what Robbie, Philip, or Grandpa said. Then go on. Answers may vary. Encourage students to explain their answers.

EXTEND

Students will have a good idea of what is going to happen in this episode. Ask students what they think each of the characters will do.

What will Albert do?

What will Philip do?

Robbie? Grandpa?

ACT II
VIDEO GAMES

Scene 1: "I just saw a big one!"

LISTEN IN

SOUND ON

8:45 - 10:36

Read the statements below. Then watch the scene and listen to it carefully. Which of the following items are true according to the information in the scene? Put a check (✔) in the box only if you are sure the sentence is true.

☐ 1. Robbie is hungry.

☐ 2. Philip has fished in this lake before.

☐ 3. Grandpa taught Philip how to fish.

☐ 4. There are big fish in this lake.

☐ 5. Albert is ten years old.

☐ 6. Albert is on vacation.

☐ 7. Albert's father is at the lodge.

☐ 8. Albert doesn't know how to swim.

☐ 9. Philip is worried about Albert.

☐ 10. The water in the lake is deep.

☐ 11. Albert is not a good fisherman.

☐ 12. It is going to rain soon.

WITH THE WHOLE CLASS

THE SUBTEXT

1 Robbie: I'm hungry.

2 Philip: I'm afraid he might fall into the water.

3 Grandpa: Shouldn't you be here with an adult?

Read Philip's, Grandpa's, and Robbie's thoughts above. Then watch the scene again and listen to the men's conversation. What do the characters say to express these thoughts? Tell your teacher to stop the tape when you hear each answer.

Scene 2: "See, it works!"

WHAT'S GOING ON?

IN SMALL GROUPS

SOUND ON
PICTURE OFF

10:37 - 12:23

With the picture off, listen to the scene. Try to guess the action. Read each paragraph below. With your group, choose the correct story. Circle the number of your group's choice.

1. Grandpa tells Robbie his magic way to catch a fish. When he turns his hat around, it drops into the water. Robbie repeats the magic words and catches a fish. With his fishing rod, Philip is able to get Grandpa's hat out of the water. The men decide to build a fire to dry the hat. They ask Albert to join them, but he wants to keep fishing.

2. Grandpa tells Robbie his magic way to catch a fish. Robbie repeats the magic words and catches a big fish. Grandpa can't get Robbie's fish into the net, but then Philip catches a fish. The men decide to build a fire to cook the fish for lunch. They ask Albert to join them, but he wants to keep fishing.

3. Grandpa tells Robbie his magic way to catch a fish. Robbie repeats the magic words and catches a big fish. Philip feels something on his fishing line, too. But when he pulls it out of the water, there is a boot on the line. The men ask Albert to help them build a fire, but he wants to keep fishing.

Now, <u>with the picture on</u>, watch the scene to check your answer.

UNDERSTUDIES

IN GROUPS OF THREE

SOUND ON

10:37 - 12:23

Watch the scene again and listen to it carefully. Work in groups of three to act out the scene. It is not important to repeat Grandpa's, Philip's, and Robbie's words exactly. Include the following information:

GRANDPA	PHILIP	ROBBIE
• teaches Robbie his magic way to catch a fish	• tells Robbie he wants to catch his lunch, not buy it	• says he wants to buy lunch
• says the magic words	• asks Grandpa to say the magic words	• repeats the magic words
	• catches a boot	• feels a fish on the line
	• invites Albert to help them build a fire for cooking	• asks Grandpa to get the net
		• tells Philip that Philip forgot to say the magic words

After you practice the scene, you may perform it for the whole class.

WHAT'S GOING ON?

PREPARE
Pre-teach: *fishing line, fishing net, boot.*

PARTICIPATE
1. With the class, read the instruction line and paragraphs 1–3.
2. Turn the picture off and play scene 2 (10:37 to 12:23).
3. Have students complete the exercise.
4. Turn the picture on and play scene 2 again.
5. Review student answers.

UNDERSTUDIES

PREPARE
1. Pre-teach: *It works* (It's effective), *You bet* (You're right).
2. Assemble the following props: three pointers or rulers and some string as fishing poles, a hat, a paper fish, a boot or shoe.

PARTICIPATE
1. Divide the class into groups of three, A, B, and C.
2. With the class, read the instruction line and the actions that Grandpa, Philip, and Robbie perform in the scene.
3. Ask students to choose a character.
4. Play scene 2 again.
5. Taking the characters one at a time, elicit the dialogue. Allow for variations. Encourage students to use their own ideas. Avoid repeating the actual dialogue word for word. Replay scene 2, if necessary.
6. Have the groups practice the dialogue.
7. Ask for a volunteer group to perform the scene for the class. Ask for other groups to volunteer. Allow as many groups as wish to volunteer to do so.

EXTEND
1. Write this scene change on the board: Philip hooks a car tire and falls in the water. Then Ellen, Marilyn, and Susan arrive.
2. Organize groups of three to play Ellen, Marilyn, and Susan.
3. Seat the new groups and the old groups together to work out new dialogue. Hint: Maybe the women have had better luck fishing.
4. Ask for volunteers to act the new scene in front of the class.

WHAT IS HE SAYING?

PREPARE
Pre-teach: *rare, medium, well-done, burned, help!* (distress call), *easy does it, to breathe.*

PARTICIPATE
1. With the class, read the instruction line and the words beneath the photos.
2. Turn the sound off and play scene 3 (12:24 to 13:34).
3. Have students complete the exercise.
4. Turn the sound on and play scene 3 again.
5. Review student answers.

FREEZE!

PARTICIPATE
1. Pre-teach: *to drown, mouth to mouth resuscitation, to survive.*
2. Ask the class:
   Does Albert know how to swim?
   Does Robbie?
   How long was Albert in the water?
   What is Philip doing to save his life?

FOCUS IN: DESCRIBING A SEQUENCE

PREPARE
1. Pre-teach these time expressions and write them on the board: *first, next, then, after that, later on, finally, last.*
2. To introduce your class to the concept of describing a sequence, mime a sequence of actions in the classroom for them. Have students watch you carefully and remember your actions.
   a. Open the door.
   b. Look outside.
   c. Close the door.
3. Using the cue words on the board, ask students to tell you the sequence:
   First, you opened the door.
   Then, you looked outside.
   Last, you closed the door.
4. Mime a sequence of five classroom actions and elicit the sequence from your students using the cue words *first, next, after that, later on, finally.*

PARTICIPATE
Watch the "Focus In" segment (13:35 to 15:36).

STORYTELLER
1. Divide the class into small groups.
2. With the class, read the instruction line.
3. Have students choose a member of their group to retell the story.

STORYWRITER
1. With the class, read the instruction line.
2. Have students complete the exercise.

Scene 3: "Breathe, Albert!"

WHAT IS HE SAYING?

SOUND OFF

12:24 - 13:34

With the sound off, watch the scene. Look for the three scenes in the pictures below. What is Philip saying? Circle a, b, or c.

Philip: a. Do you like your fish rare, medium, or well done?
b. I hope you like your fish well done.
c. I'm sorry I burned this fish.

Philip: a. Easy does it, Robbie.
b. Never mind, Robbie. I can do it alone.
c. Help me lift him out of the water, Son.

Philip: a. Robbie, find his father right now!
b. Robbie, call an ambulance right away!
c. Robbie, run to the car! Bring a blanket and my medical bag.

Now, **with the sound on,** watch the scene to check your answers.

FREEZE!

WITH THE WHOLE CLASS

PAUSE AT 13:34

Will Albert survive? Tell your opinions. You will find out the answer in Act III!

IN SMALL GROUPS

ACT II
DESCRIBING A SEQUENCE

SOUND ON

13:35 - 15:36

Watch the "Focus In" segment. Then do the activities below.

STORYTELLER	WORD BOX	STORYWRITERS
Choose one student from your group to retell the story of Act II to the rest of the class. Help him or her to remember the details. Use the words and expressions from the Word Box.	First . . . Next . . . Then . . . After that . . . Later on . . . Finally . . . Last . . .	With your group, write the whole story of Act II. Choose one member of your group to be the secretary. Use the words and expressions from the Word Box.

IN OTHER WORDS...

SOUND ON

16:17 - 18:07

Which word or phrase do the characters use to express each of the following meanings? Watch the scene again to find the answers. When you hear the correct word or phrase, write it on the line next to the meaning.

1. a wonderful man _____
2. thankful _____
3. Good-bye _____
4. Let's . . . _____
5. There's a problem. _____

Scene 2: "We had a good day."

SPLIT DIALOGUE

IN GROUPS OF THREE

SOUND ON

18:08 - 19:09

Watch the scene to complete the sentences below. Work with two other students. One of you will complete Ellen's lines; one will complete Grandpa's; the third student will complete Robbie's. Choose the correct words from the Word Box. Play the scene as many times as necessary.

ELLEN	GRANDPA	ROBBIE	WORD BOX
1. Why are you _____ so early?	1. Philip _____ to go back to the _____.	1. He had an _____.	caught did down really good great back bad know out had saved emergency water doctor fun special hospital
2. Oh, that's too _____, Robbie. Did it spoil your _____?	2. We had a _____ day. Robbie pulled a boy _____ of the _____.	2. No, Mom. We had a _____ time.	
3. Well, _____ you do any fishing?		3. Yeah, we _____ lots of them. Look! They had a _____ on frozen fish _____ at the supermarket.	
4. Oh, you _____ had a bad day.		4. And Dad _____ his life. He's a terrific _____, Mom.	
5. I _____.			

Now watch the scene again. Check your answers with your group. Then practice reading the dialogue together.

IN OTHER WORDS...

PREPARE
Pre-teach: *to wrap* (something), *quite a guy, so long* (good-bye), *patient*.

PARTICIPATE
1. Divide the class into pairs, A and B.
2. With the class, read the instruction line and expressions 1–5.
3. Replay scene 1.
4. Have students complete the exercise.
5. Replay scene 1, if necessary.
6. Review answers.

SPLIT DIALOGUE

PREPARE
Pre-teach from the Word Box: *emergency, special, to save* (someone's life).

PARTICIPATE
1. Divide the class into groups of three, A, B, and C.
2. With the class, read the instruction line and review the words in the Word Box.
3. Play scene 2 (18:08 to 19:09).
4. Have students complete the exercise. *Note:* For pairs of more advanced levels, each student may be able to complete more than one character's dialogue in the time allotted.
5. Replay scene 2.
6. Review student answers.

FURTHER PRACTICE
1. Have the groups practice their three-part dialogue.
2. Ask for student volunteers to play the scene in front of the class.

EXTEND
As one of the volunteer groups is finishing the scene, surprise them by walking on stage as Philip and saying, "Well, I'm back from the hospital. What's for dinner tonight?" Continue the scene. Try to get the students to improvise dialogue.

LISTEN IN

PREPARE
Pre-teach: *pop* (father), *schedule*.

PARTICIPATE
1. With the class, read the instruction line and statements 1–9 below.
2. Play scene 3 (19:10 to 20:39).
3. Have students complete the exercise on their own.
4. Review student answers.
5. Replay the scene to check answers.

EXTEND
Discuss: Does Grandpa really have other plans, or does he want to let Philip and Robbie have a day together with just the two of them? Will he change his mind and go fishing?

Scene 3: "Why don't we do it again?"

LISTEN IN

SOUND ON
19:10 - 20:39

Read the statements below. Then watch the scene and listen to it carefully. Which of the following items are true according to the information in the scene? Put a check (✔) in the box only if you are sure the sentence is true.

☐ 1. Philip is tired this evening.

☐ 2. Philip's patient will be OK.

☐ 3. Robbie is thinking about becoming a doctor.

☐ 4. Philip wanted to be a doctor when he was Robbie's age.

☐ 5. Philip wants to go fishing again next Saturday.

☐ 6. Robbie agrees to go.

☐ 7. Robbie wants Grandpa to go fishing with them.

☐ 8. Grandpa wants Philip and Robbie to spend time alone.

☐ 9. Grandpa is going to learn how to use the computer.

ACT III *Focus In*

MAKING SUGGESTIONS

SOUND ON

20:40- 22:41

WITH THE WHOLE CLASS

A. Watch the "Focus In" segment. Then watch it again and sing along. Here are the words to the song.

Philip: Maybe we can spend some time together next weekend.

Maybe . . .
Maybe . . .
Maybe we can spend some time together.
Maybe we can stay at home,
Maybe get away.
Oh, yeah!
'Cause I really like to be with you.
I know we'll have fun
Whatever we do.
And maybe we can do it again another day.

Maybe we can go bowling.
And golf would be fun to play.
Maybe we can play baseball,
Or go fishing on a summer—
Fishing on a summer day!

Grandpa: What do you say we get back to our fishing?

What do you say . . .
What do you say . . .
What do you say we get back to our fishing?
What do you say we fish?
That's what we want to do!
So let's get back to it right away.
We don't want to waste this beautiful day.
What do you say we keep on fishing till the day is through?

Philip. Why don't we do it again!

Why don't we do it . . .
Why don't we do it . . .
Why don't we do it again?
Why don't we find the time?
Hey, what do you say?
There are lots of things that we can do.
And I enjoy spending time with you.
So why don't we do it again another day?

IN SMALL GROUPS

B. Make some suggestions for each situation below. Use the expressions from the Conversation Box.

1. Suggest ideas for a big party on Saturday night.
2. Suggest things you can do to help the environment.
3. Suggest ways to improve your English.

CONVERSATION BOX

Maybe (we) can (+ simple verb)

Maybe (we) could (+ simple verb)

Maybe (we) should (+ simple verb)

What do you say we (+ simple verb)

Why don't we (+ simple verb)

Let's (+ simple verb)

How about (+ *-ing* verb)

FOCUS IN: MAKING SUGGESTIONS

PREPARE
Pre-teach: *bowling, golf, to waste, to keep on, through* (finished).

PARTICIPATE
1. With the class, read instruction line A.
2. Play the "Focus In" segment (20:40 to 22:41).
3. Play the segment again and sing along.
4. Divide the class into small groups.
5. With the class, read instruction line B and review the expressions in the Conversation Box.
6. Have students complete the exercise. Designate one student in each group to take notes.
7. Ask for student volunteers to read some of their suggestions to the class.

ACT III FINALE
USEFUL LANGUAGE

PREPARE
Read through and explain the expressions to your students.

PARTICIPATE
1. Have students close their books.
2. Make the statements below. Elicit responses from the class. The possible student answers are in parentheses.

Teacher: We all enjoyed singing that song.
Student: (Why don't we sing the song again? *or* What do you say we sing the song again?)
Teacher: I'm leaving. Good-bye.
Student: (So long.)
Teacher: You spilled coffee on me.
Student: (I'm sorry. I guess I ruined your day.)
Teacher: My father raised seven children all by himself.
Student: (Your dad is quite a guy.)
Teacher: I have some bad news for you.
Student: (Uh-oh.)
Teacher: He/she (indicate a student) just saved your house from burning down.
Student: (How can I thank you? *or* I'm so thankful to you.

U.S. LIFE

PREPARE
Pre-teach: *superstition, belief, to knock, four-leaf clover, horseshoe, ladder, mirror, to avoid, sign* (indication).

PARTICIPATE
1. Have students read independently.
2. Ask:
   a. Name three things that bring good luck.
   b. Name two things that bring bad luck.

YOUR TURN
Complete this exercise in small groups or with the entire class.

ACT III
FINALE

USEFUL LANGUAGE

In Act III, you heard ways to . . .

• make suggestions:
What do you say we get back to our fishing?
Why don't we do it again?

• say good-bye informally:
So long.

• say you admire someone:
Your dad is quite a guy.

• react to bad news:
Uh-oh.

• express thanks:
How can I thank all of you?
I'm very grateful . . .
I'm so thankful to all of you.

• apologize:
I guess I ruined your day.

READ AND DISCUSS

Read the paragraphs under "U.S. Life." Then discuss your answers to the questions under "Your Turn."

ON YOUR OWN

U.S. LIFE

Most Americans probably don't believe that actions like Grandpa's "fisherman's magic" will affect their lives. Grandpa tells Robbie that to catch a fish, he should say, "Fish, fish, send me a fish." This is a **superstition**, a belief that something brings good or bad luck—without a scientific reason to think so. But there are some traditional signs of good luck and bad luck in the U.S., and Americans *do* pay attention to them sometimes.

People sometimes say that the following actions bring good luck:

knocking on wood
finding a four-leaf clover
carrying a rabbit's foot
hanging a horseshoe over your door

Some people believe that these events cause bad luck:

walking under a ladder
breaking a mirror
seeing a black cat cross in front of you

Although people may say that they don't believe in these superstitions, they often try to avoid the signs of bad luck and are happy to have a sign of good luck.

IN SMALL GROUPS

YOUR TURN

1. What are some common superstitions in your country? Do you believe in them?
2. Can you tell about a time when you felt lucky—or unlucky?

knocking on wood

a four-leaf clover

a rabbit's foot

a horseshoe

walking under a ladder   breaking a mirror

seeing a black cat cross in front of you

ACT I
INTERMISSION

PRONUNCIATION: the letter c

- The letter *c* usually sounds like *s* when it comes before the letters *i, e,* and *y.*
  EXAMPLES: cinnamon / spice / cent / bicycle

  Otherwise, *c* sounds like *k.*
  EXAMPLES: care / act / cut
- The letters *cc* before *i* or before *e* sound like *ks.*
  EXAMPLES: accident / success

  Otherwise, *cc* sounds like *k.*
  EXAMPLE: occupation

What is the sound of *c* or *cc* in each of the following words? Write *s, k,* or *ks* in the box below each word. Then pronounce each word correctly.

1. cabinet   **2.** grocer   **3.** accountant   **4.** accent   **5.** according

□   □   □   □   □

USEFUL LANGUAGE

In Act I, you heard ways to . . .

- tell someone to begin working:
  We should get to work.
  Come on, Philip! Get busy with your famous apple pie.
- talk about possibilities:
  Is it possible that we forgot to buy cinnamon?

- ask someone for help:
  Can you do me a favor?
- praise a child:
  That's my boy!

- wish someone a happy holiday:
  Happy Thanksgiving to you and your family.
- ask why someone is acting strangely:
  What's gotten into him?

IN GROUPS OF THREE

INSTANT ROLE-PLAYS

Practice this conversation with two other students.

At home on Saturday afternoon . . .

Mom: I have such a headache! Is it possible that we ran out of aspirin?
Dad: Can you do me a favor?
Child: Sure, Dad.
Dad: Could you go to the drugstore and get some aspirin for your mother?
Child: I'll go right away.
Dad: That's my boy/girl!

Then practice this conversation.

On a camping trip . . .

A: It's getting dark. We should get busy and build a campfire.
B: Where are the matches?
C: If there are any matches, they're in the backpack, with the first-aid kit.
A: Is it possible that we forgot to take matches?
B: They're not here. How can we make a fire without matches?
C: Do me a favor. Walk back to the country store and get some.
B: Not me. It's too dark.

ACT I INTERMISSION
PRONUNCIATION: THE LETTER C

PARTICIPATE
1. With the class, read the explanation and examples.
2. Have students complete the exercise.
3. Review student answers.

USEFUL LANGUAGE

PREPARE
Read through and explain the expressions to your students.

PARTICIPATE
1. Have students close their books.
2. Make the statements below. Elicit responses from the class. The possible student answers are in parentheses.

Teacher: I'm going to spend Thanksgiving with my family.
Student: (Happy Thanksgiving to you and your family.)
Teacher: It's getting late. We have to finish this episode today.
Student: (We should get to work. *or* Come on, let's get busy with this episode.)
Teacher: You know what? I don't have my keys.
Student: (Answers employing *possibility* expressions.)
Teacher: We used to go camping all the time.
Student: (Maybe we should do it again.)
Teacher: My dog suddenly ran away from home.
Student: (What's gotten into him?)

INSTANT ROLE-PLAYS

PREPARE
Pre-teach: *headache, aspirin, drugstore, backpack, first-aid kit.*

PARTICIPATE
1. Divide the class into groups of three, A, B, and C.
2. Have students complete the exercise.

LESSON TWO

ACT II PREVIEW

PREPARE
Pre-teach: *parade, to cheer up* (someone), *float, clown, kids, to come on* (television).

PARTICIPATE
1. With the class, read the instruction line, questions 1–5, and the words in the Answer Box.
2. Play the Preview (33:23 to 33:51).
3. Have students complete the exercise.
4. Replay the Preview, if necessary.
5. Review student answers.

EXTEND: IS IT ALEXANDRA?
Pair Work: Imagine it is Alexandra calling. Instruct student pairs to write a short telephone conversation between Robbie and Alexandra.

WATCH OUT

PREPARE
Review these action verbs: *to sing, to cry, to hit, to laugh, to move, to jump, to point.*

PARTICIPATE
1. With the class, read the instruction line and statements 1–9.
2. Turn off the sound and play scene 1 (33:52 to 34:50).
3. Have students complete the exercise on their own.
4. Review student answers.
5. Replay the scene to check answers.

ACT II
PREVIEW

SOUND ON

33:23 - 33:51

Read the following questions. Then watch the preview to find the answers. Choose your answers from the Answer Box. Write the answers on the blank lines.

1. What are Grandpa and Robbie watching on TV?_____
2. What two things does Grandpa point to?_____
3. What is Philip excited about? _____
4. Which team is playing in the football game today? _____
5. What is Robbie expecting? _____

> **ANSWER BOX**
> a football game
> a float
> a telephone call
> a parade
> clowns
> Michigan

ACT II
VIDEO GAMES

Scene 1: "I love parades."

WATCH OUT

SOUND OFF

33:52 - 34:50

Read each item below. Then, with the sound off, watch the scene. What does Grandpa do to cheer up Robbie? Put a check (✓) in the box only if the sentence tells something that Grandpa does.

☐ **1.** He sings.
☐ **2.** He cries.
☐ **3.** He hits Robbie's leg.
☐ **4.** He laughs.
☐ **5.** He moves his legs.
☐ **6.** He jumps.
☐ **7.** He talks seriously.
☐ **8.** He points at the TV.
☐ **9.** He tells funny stories.

LISTEN IN

SOUND ON

33:52 - 34:50

Read each item below. Then, with the sound on, watch the scene. Which of the following items does Grandpa talk about to cheer up Robbie? Put a check (✔) in the box <u>only if Grandpa mentions the item.</u>

☐	1. a Superman balloon	☐ 4. a crowd of people laughing	☐ 7. a float
☐	2. a policeman	☐ 5. a television crew	☐ 8. an old car
☐	3. a band	☐ 6. Central Park	☐ 9. some clowns

Scene 2: "He'll get over it."

ON THE PHONE

IN PAIRS

SOUND ON

34:51 - 35:24

Watch the scene. Listen to Ellen's conversation with Susan. With your partner, try to guess Susan's part of the conversation. What did she say to Ellen? Circle *a* or *b* for each of Susan's lines below. Then practice reading the "correct" conversation with your partner.

Ellen: Hello, Susan.

Susan: **a.** Hi. What's gotten into Robbie?
b. Hi. Is Robbie upset about something?

Ellen: Yes, he missed a phone call from Alexandra.

Susan: **a.** Is that all?
b. He sounds terrible.

Ellen: Yes, I know, but he'll get over it.

Susan: **a.** What time should we come to dinner?
b. We'll be leaving at four o'clock.

Ellen: Good. Then you'll be here about five?

Susan: **a.** Yes. Should we bring anything?
b. Uh-huh.

Ellen: Oh, fine. I look forward to seeing you and Harry and Michelle.

Susan: **a.** We can't wait to see you!
b. See you tomorrow.

Ellen: Drive carefully. Good-bye.

LISTEN IN

PREPARE

1. Pre-teach: *Superman, balloon, wowee!* (exclamation of awe). Using a map of New York City, show the Thanksgiving Day Parade route along Central Park West.
2. CULTURE NOTE: Since 1924, Macy's department store in New York has organized the Thanksgiving Day Parade. The parade features floats, large balloons of TV and cartoon characters, and marching bands. The bands play the music of famous American composers like John Philip Sousa.

PARTICIPATE

1. With the class, read the instruction line and items 1–9 below.
2. Turn on the sound and replay scene 1 (33:52 to 34:50).
3. Have students complete the exercise on their own.
4. Review student answers.
5. Replay the scene to check answers.

ON THE PHONE

PREPARE

Pre-teach: *to get over* (recover from) *something, to look forward to.*

PARTICIPATE

1. Divide the class into pairs, A and B.
2. With the class, read the instruction line.
3. Play scene 2 (34:51 to 35:24).
4. With the class, read the conversation between Ellen and Susan.
5. Replay the scene, if necessary.
6. Have students complete the exercise.
7. Review student answers.

EXTEND

Conversation: Student pairs assume the roles of Ellen and Philip. Ellen repeats the information from the phone call:

When Susan is arriving.

Who she is bringing with her.

UNDERSTUDIES

PREPARE

1. Pre-teach: *turkey dressing, recipe, wrong number* (person telephoning by mistake), *to serve* (food), *to remind.*
2. CULTURE NOTE: Thanksgiving football games are played between rival universities. In this episode, Philip's alma mater, the University of Michigan, is one of the teams playing.

PARTICIPATE

1. Divide the class into groups of four, A, B, C, and D.
2. With the class, read instruction line A and the actions that Philip, Grandpa, Robbie, and Ellen perform in the scene.
3. Ask students to choose a character.
4. Turn the sound off and play the scene segment (35:25 to 36:20).
5. Ask for a group to volunteer to walk through the actions at the front of the room. Provide the bowl and spoon as props. *Note:* Actions only, no words. Standardize the actions. Ask for another group to volunteer. Allow as many groups as wish to volunteer to do so.
6. With the class, read instruction line B and the actions that Philip, Grandpa, Robbie, and Ellen perform in the scene.
7. Turn the sound on and replay the scene segment.
8. Taking the characters one at a time, elicit the dialogue. Allow for variations. Encourage students to use their own ideas. Avoid repeating the actual dialogue word for word.
9. Have the groups practice the dialogue.
10. With the class, read instruction line C. Ask for a volunteer group to perform actions and dialogue for the class. Ask for other groups to volunteer. Allow as many groups as wish to volunteer to do so.

Scene 3: "Is it for me?"
UNDERSTUDIES

IN GROUPS OF FOUR

SOUND OFF

35:25 - 36:20

A. With the sound off, watch this part of the scene. Work in groups of four to perform only the *actions* in the scene. Include these events:

PHILIP	GRANDPA	ROBBIE	ELLEN
• walks into the room	• tries some turkey dressing	• tries some turkey dressing	• walks into the room
• offers turkey dressing to Grandpa		• listens when the phone rings	• walks out of the room
• offers turkey dressing to Robbie			
• sits down to watch TV			
• leaves the room			
• comes back into the room			

SOUND ON

35:25 - 36:20

B. Now, with the sound on, watch this part of the scene again. Work with your group to say the following information. It is not important to repeat the characters' words exactly.

PHILIP	GRANDPA	ROBBIE	ELLEN
• offers some turkey dressing	• says it's Grandma's recipe	• says the dressing is his favorite part of the meal	• says the phone call was a wrong number
• asks Robbie about his apple pie	• says Ellen reminds him of Grandma	• says Philip's apple pie is his favorite dessert	• asks Philip to return to the kitchen
• asks about the parade		• asks if the phone call is for him	• tells Robbie to relax with Grandpa
• asks the time of the football game		• offers to help Ellen	• calls Philip
• says he'll be back to watch the game			

C. Put together the actions and dialogue from Parts A and B. Practice the scene three times. Then perform it for the whole class.

WHEN DID IT HAPPEN?

SOUND ON

36:21 - 36:53

With the sound on, watch the end of the scene to answer the questions. Write the answers in complete sentences on the lines below.

1. When did Philip graduate from college? _____
2. When did Philip graduate from medical school? _____
3. When did Grandpa graduate from college? _____

WITH THE WHOLE CLASS

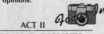

FREEZE!

PAUSE AT 36:48

What is Grandpa laughing about? Discuss your opinions.

ACT II

LIKES AND DISLIKES

ON YOUR OWN

SOUND ON

36:54 - 38:54

A. Watch the "Focus In" segment. Then list your own likes and dislikes on the lines below.

I like . . .	I dislike . . .
_____	_____
_____	_____
_____	_____
_____	_____

IN SMALL GROUPS

B. Now tell your group about your likes and dislikes. The other members of your group will ask you to explain your reasons. Use the expressions from the Conversation Box.

CONVERSATION BOX

I like	I don't like	Why do you like _____ so much?
I love . . .	I dislike . . .	Why don't you like _____?
I enjoy . . .	I hate . . .	
I'm fond of . . .	I can't stand . . .	
I'm crazy about . . .		
I'm wild about . . .		

WHEN DID IT HAPPEN?

PREPARE

Pre-teach: *to graduate, medical school, yep* (informal "yes").

PARTICIPATE

1. With the class, read the instruction line and questions 1–3.
2. Turn the sound off and play the scene segment (36:21 to 36:53).
3. Have students complete the exercise.
4. Replay the scene segment to check answers.
5. Review student answers.

FREEZE!

PARTICIPATE

1. Pause the video at 36:48.
2. Ask students:
   Grandpa is laughing because:
   a. He enjoys seeing Robbie in love.
   b. He enjoys seeing Robbie unhappy.
   c. He enjoys seeing Robbie experience life.
3. Discuss answers.

FOCUS IN: LIKES AND DISLIKES

PREPARE

Pre-teach the expressions in the Conversation Box.

PARTICIPATE

1. With the class, read instruction line A.
2. Watch the "Focus In" segment (36:54 to 38:54).
3. Have students complete the exercise. If they have trouble getting ideas, tell them to think about their weekly routines. What activities do they like? What activities do they dislike?
4. Divide the class into small groups.
5. With the class, read instruction line B.
6. Have students complete the exercise.

EXTEND

Discuss: Ask students to tell the class about a spouse, roommate, or close friend. What are their likes and dislikes? Does this make them easy or difficult to get along with?

ACT II INTERMISSION
USEFUL LANGUAGE

PREPARE
Read through and explain the expressions to your students.

PARTICIPATE
1. Have students close their books.
2. Make the statements below. Elicit responses from the class. The possible student answers are in parentheses.

Teacher: My son's cat got sick and died. My son is very sad.
Student: (That's too bad. Don't worry, he'll get over it.)
Teacher: How do you feel about your vacation next week?
Student: (I'm looking forward to it.)
Teacher: It's possible Alexandra is Robbie's first girlfriend.
Student: (Maybe so.)
Teacher: How do you feel about getting up early in the morning? vacations at the seashore? scary movies? doing dishes? studying English?
Student: (Answers will vary.)
Teacher: Look out the window of our airplane. We're flying over New York City. Isn't it great?
Student: (Wowee!)

INSTANT ROLE-PLAYS

PREPARE
Pre-teach: *to get fired* (from a job).

PARTICIPATE
Repeat the role-play procedure outlined on page 7.

U.S. LIFE

PREPARE
Pre-teach: *Pilgrims, yams, pumpkin pie.*

PARTICIPATE
1. Have students read independently.
2. Ask:
   a. In what year was the first Thanksgiving celebrated?
   b. Name two other holidays with large parades.

YOUR TURN

Complete this exercise in small groups or with the entire class.

ACT II
INTERMISSION

USEFUL LANGUAGE

In Act II, you heard ways to . . .

- express enthusiasm: *Look at that Superman balloon! Wowee!*
- agree that something is possible: *Maybe so.*

- say someone will recover: *He'll get over it.*
- express happiness about a future event: *I look forward to seeing you . . .*

- express likes/dislikes: *I love parades.*
- say yes informally: *Yup.*

↕

IN PAIRS

INSTANT ROLE-PLAYS

Practice this conversation with a partner.

At the office . . .

A: Anthony is grouchy today.
B: What's wrong with him?
A: He was looking forward to getting a pay raise.
B: You mean he didn't get it?
A: No. In fact, he almost got fired.
B: I guess we should get to work.

Then complete this conversation:

On a plane to California . . .

A: Just look at those mountains! Wowee! I love flying.
B:
A:
B:
A:
B:

READ AND DISCUSS

Read the paragraphs under "U.S. Life." Then discuss your answers to the questions under "Your Turn."

ON YOUR OWN

U.S. LIFE

Americans of all religions celebrate **Thanksgiving**, a happy holiday on the fourth Thursday of each November. This holiday began with the **Pilgrims**. The Pilgrims celebrated the first Thanksgiving in Plymouth, Massachusetts, in 1621. Americans still get together on this day to remember the reasons to be thankful. Families and friends celebrate this holiday with big dinners of turkey, turkey dressing, yams and other vegetables, and pumpkin pie.

Parades are also a part of the Thanksgiving holiday. Each year, Macy's, the largest store in the world, organizes the **Thanksgiving Day parade** in New York City.

Parades are also a big part of other American holidays. Some of the largest parades occur on Columbus Day (the second Monday in October), Veterans Day (November 11), Independence Day (July 4), and Labor Day (the first Monday in September).

IN SMALL GROUPS
YOUR TURN

1. Is there a holiday like Thanksgiving in your country? What are the traditional activities on that day?
2. Do you enjoy watching parades? If so, what do you like most about them?

ACT III
PREVIEW
SOUND OFF

39:00 - 39:41

With the sound off, watch the preview. Pause at the four times below. What are the characters saying? Can you guess? For each time you pause, choose the correct speech balloon at the bottom of the page. Then write the letter of the correct answer inside each television screen.

1. [ ]   2. [ ]   3. [ ]   4. [ ]

PAUSE AT 39:11   PAUSE AT 39:25   PAUSE AT 39:32   PAUSE AT 39:36

a. *Did you forget something?*

c. *And I'd also like to thank my math teacher for giving me a passing grade.*

b. *Remember, the Michigan football game? And Michigan needs a touchdown.*

d. *Then in that spirit let's each of us give thanks. Each in his own way.*

Now, <u>with the sound on</u>, watch the preview to check your answers.

ACT III
VIDEO GAMES
Scene 1: "Let's each of us give thanks."
AROUND THE TABLE
SOUND ON

39:42 - 41:50

A. Watch scene 1. Listen carefully to what each member of the family gives thanks for. Then write the correct name before each phrase below. The first answer is given.

1. *Grandpa*: for being with the family
2. _____: for being well
3. _____: for a healthy year
4. _____: for a good job
5. _____: for meeting Harry and Michelle
6. _____: for meeting Susan
7. _____: for meeting the Stewart Family
8. _____: for Grandpa coming to live with the family
9. _____: for a passing grade in math
10. _____: for a patient wife
11. _____: for an encouraging husband
12. _____: for the food on the table

IN SMALL GROUPS

B. You are visiting the Stewart Family for Thanksgiving dinner. Now it's your turn. What will you give thanks for? Tell your group.

LESSON THREE
ACT III PREVIEW

PREPARE

Pre-teach: *to give thanks, spirit* (feeling), *in his/her own way* (in his/her personal style), *grade* (mark), *touchdown*.

PARTICIPATE

1. With the class, read the instruction line and the dialogue in the speech balloons.
2. Turn the sound off and play the Preview (39:00 to 39:41).
3. Have students complete the exercise.
4. Turn the sound on and replay the Preview to check answers.

EXTEND: WHAT DID PHILIP FORGET?
Hint: Something is wrong with Philip's famous apple pie.

AROUND THE TABLE
PREPARE

1. Pre-teach: *call me* _____ (use my first name), *to take a moment* (pause for a moment), *meaning, school play, harvest, Indians* (Native Americans), *to give thanks* (for something), *healthy, patient* (unhurried), *to encourage, to go along with something* (to agree with something).
2. CULTURE NOTE: It is customary to tap a water glass at a dinner gathering to get people's attention if we want to make a speech.

PARTICIPATE

1. Divide the class into small groups.
2. With the class, read instruction line A and phrases 1–12 below.
3. With books closed, play scene 1 (39:42 to 41:50).
4. Have students open their books and complete the exercise.
5. Replay scene 1 to check answers.
6. With the class, read instruction line B.
7. Elicit expressions of thanks from the students.

GROUP DIALOGUE

PRFPARF

Pre-teach: *score* (of a game), *break* (rest).

PARTICIPATE

1. With the class, read the instruction line and the words in the Word Box.
2. With books closed, play scene 2 (41:51 to 42:35).
3. Have students open their books and complete the exercise.
4. Replay scene 2, if necessary.
5. Review answers.

SUMMARY

PREPARE

Pre-teach: *in the meantime.*

PARTICIPATE

1. With the class, read the instruction line and the summary below.
2. With books closed, turn the sound off and play scene 3 (42:36 to 44:28).
3. Have students open their books and complete the exercise.
4. Replay scene 3, if necessary.
5. Review student answers.

FURTHER PRACTICE

1. Have the groups practice a three-part dialogue.
2. Ask for student volunteers to play the scene in front of the class.

Scene 2: "And Michigan needs a touchdown."

GROUP DIALOGUE

SOUND ON

41:51 - 42:35

Watch the scene to complete the sentences below. Choose the correct words from the Word Box. Write the words on the blank lines. Play the scene as many times as necessary.

Harry: It was a _____ meal, Mrs. Stewart. Thank you.
Richard: And now to see the _____ of the football game.
Philip: Exactly.
Ellen: _____ are you _____, Philip?
Philip: Remember, the Michigan _____ game? And Michigan _____ a touchdown
Ellen: Did you _____ something?
Robbie: Dad, your _____ apple pie.
Philip: Just _____ me see the score, Ellen.
Marilyn: Go _____, Philip. We should all take a little break before dessert.

(The doorbell rings.)

Ellen: Oh, who _____ that be? Oh, it must be Alexandra. I invited her to come _____ for dessert.
Robbie: You _____?
Grandpa: I _____ Ellen.

WORD BOX
going
ahead
needs
forget
football
did
Where
like
let
wonderful
by
could
famous
end

Scene 3: "You know everyone, Alexandra."

SUMMARY

SOUND OFF

42:36 - 44:28

Read the following summary of the action in this scene. Then, with the sound off, watch the scene to fill in the missing information.

Alexandra arrived after dinner. Robbie took her _____. Ellen introduced her to _____ and _____. Alexandra brought a dessert for the Stewarts. She sat down at the _____. _____ and _____ came in from the living room to greet her. _____ ran back to watch the rest of the game. Philip went to look in the _____. He forgot to do something, and then he went back to the living room. Alexandra talked with _____. Then _____ sat down next to her. In the meantime, Philip and Richard were watching the football game as Michigan player number _____ ran for a touchdown. Grandpa said it was a great Thanksgiving.

IN FACT

IN PAIRS

SOUND ON

42:36 - 44:28

Now, with the sound on, watch the scene. Complete this activity with a partner. Take turns asking and answering the questions. If your answer is *no*, give the correct answer. The first answer is given.

1. Did Alexandra bring an apple pie?
   No, she didn't. She brought a pumpkin pie.
2. Are there two minutes left to play in the football game?

3. Did Philip forget to turn on the oven?

4. Did Alexandra spend the day with the Stewart family?

ACT III
THANKSGIVING

SOUND ON

44:29 - 46:29

Watch the "Focus In" segment to complete these sentences about the holiday.

1. The first Thanksgiving was in _____.
2. Thanksgiving was about the _____, the first settlers.
3. They shared the first _____ with the _____ and gave thanks.
4. Thanksgiving is a day with many _____.
5. People eat traditional foods, like _____ and _____ and fruit pies, like apple pie and _____ pie.
6. And people watch the afternoon _____ _____.

IN FACT

PREPARE
Pre-teach: *How did you guess?* (It's obvious), *oven*.

PARTICIPATE
1. Divide the class into pairs, A and B.
2. With the class, read the instruction line and questions 1–4 below.
3. Turn the sound on and replay scene 3 (42:36 to 44:28).
4. Have students complete the exercise. Have student A ask questions 1 and 2. Have student B ask questions 3 and 4.
5. Review student answers.
6. Replay the scene to check answers.

EXTEND
1. What three things does Grandpa mention at the end of Act III? Elicit answers from students and write them on the board.
2. Which one is the most important to Robbie? to Philip and Richard?

FOCUS IN: THANKSGIVING

PREPARE
Pre-teach: *to get together*.

PARTICIPATE
1. With the class, read the instruction line and sentences 1–6.
2. Play the "Focus In" segment (44:29 to 46:29).
3. Have students complete the exercise.

ACT III FINALE
USEFUL LANGUAGE

PREPARE

Read through and explain the expressions to your students.

PARTICIPATE

1. Have students close their books.
2. Make the statements below. Elicit responses from the class. The possible student answers are in parentheses.

Teacher: You know something? You're one of the best classes I've ever taught.

Student: (That was very kind of you.)

Teacher: I hope I'm being a patient teacher.

Student: (You are. I'd like to thank you for being so patient.)

Teacher: (Stand up) You know, I'm getting tired of standing up.

Student: (Please sit down.)

Teacher: I'd love a cup of coffee right now.

Student: (I'll go along with that.)

Teacher: We've been working at this episode for quite a while.

Student: (We should all take a little break.)

Teacher: You're getting a little tired, aren't you?

Student: (How'd you guess?)

Teacher: We can't take a long break.

Student: (Just let me take a short break.)

U.S. LIFE

PREPARE

Pre-teach: *typical, oblong, rectangular, object* (of a game), *goal line, round.*

PARTICIPATE

1. Have students read independently.
2. Ask:
   a. What do we call knocking a ball carrier down?
   b. What do we call the line each team tries to cross with the ball?
   c. What do we call a thrown ball?
   d. What do we call a ball kicked through goal posts?

STORYWRITER

1. With the class, read the instruction line.
2. Have those students who choose to write about their favorite sport use the text above as their model.
3. Collect writing samples and read them to the class.

YOUR TURN

Complete this exercise in small groups or with the entire class.

ACT III
FINALE

USEFUL LANGUAGE

In Act III, you heard ways to . . .

- **thank someone:**
  That was very kind of you.
  I'd like to thank Marilyn for being so patient.
- **agree:**
  I'll go along with that.
- **suggest a change in activity:**
  We should all take a little break . . .

- **say something is obvious:**
  How'd you guess?
- **say you appreciate someone's short visit:**
  I'm glad you came by.
- **thank someone for cooking:**
  It was a wonderful meal.

- **invite someone to take a seat:**
  Please sit down.
- **persuade someone to give you permission:**
  Just let me see the score . . .

READ AND DISCUSS

Read the paragraphs under "U.S. Life." Then discuss your answers to the questions under "Your Turn."

ON YOUR OWN

U.S. LIFE

Watching college football games on television is a typical Thanksgiving Day activity.

In American football, the players use an oblong ball on a rectangular playing field. There are two teams, and each team has 11 men. The object of the game is to move the ball across the opposing team's **goal line**. The opposing team tries to stop this action by knocking the ball carrier down, or **tackling** him. If the ball carrier can cross the goal line with the ball, or if he catches a thrown ball (a **pass**) and runs across the goal line, the team scores a **touchdown** and receives 6 points. If a player kicks the ball through the upright goalposts, it is called a **field goal**, and the team gets 3 points.

American football is an extremely rough sport. The players wear equipment to protect themselves, but injuries are common.

In England, the word *football* describes a different type of game with a round ball. In the U.S., this game is called *soccer*.

IN SMALL GROUPS

YOUR TURN

1. Did you ever watch an American football game? What did you think of it?
2. What is your favorite sport? Why?
3. What is the most popular sport in your country?

ON YOUR OWN

STORYWRITER

By yourself, write about one of the following:
- Describe the American Thanksgiving holiday.
- Write about your favorite sport. Why do you like it? How is it played?
- Explain in a paragraph what you would give thanks for.